Praying Through the

PSALMS

*30 Days To Uncomplicate
How You Talk to God*

Written by Shelby Dixon, Claire Foxx, Eric Gagnon, Shae Hill,
Dr. Joel Muddamalle, Michaela Payne, Meghan Ryan and Glynnis Whitwer

WE MUST EXCHANGE WHISPERS WITH GOD BEFORE SHOUTS WITH THE WORLD.

Lysa TerKeurst

PAIR YOUR STUDY GUIDE WITH THE FIRST 5 MOBILE APP!

This study guide is designed to accompany your study of Scripture in the First 5 mobile app. You can use it as a standalone study or as an accompanying guide to the daily content within First 5.

First 5 is a free mobile app developed by Proverbs 31 Ministries to transform your daily time with God.

Go to the app store on your smartphone, download the First 5 app and create a free account!

WWW.FIRST5.ORG

"Pray *without* ceasing."

That's what God's Word tells us to do in 1 Thessalonians 5:17. It's one of the shortest, simplest verses in the Bible, but if we're honest ... doesn't it seem kind of impossible?

What if your prayers feel like attempts to fill the silence in one-way conversations with a God who hears but seemingly never speaks?

What if you're used to asking God for help in hard seasons, but you're not sure what to talk to Him about the rest of the time?

What if you feel close to the Lord at church, but when you want to pray worshipful words on your own, it's not the same?

What if you finally set aside a whole hour to talk to God, but after a few minutes, your thoughts wander — then you feel guilty, so you press your palms together and close your eyes tighter and try to pray about how you wish you could pray better?

We're with you, friend. We've spent midnights staring at the ceiling and wondering why the God of the universe would even listen to what we have to say. Like you, we have journals full of questions, prayer requests and half-finished confessions interrupted by crying children, and our calendars have "prayer time" written in and then erased (more than once).

But what if ... prayer isn't meant to be this complicated?

The book of Psalms in the Old Testament is filled with prayers God has graciously given us to show it *is possible* to pray without ceasing — but only if we let go of our impossible ideas about how we're "supposed to" feel, what we're "supposed to" say, and where we're "supposed to" be when we come to Him.

As we study Psalms, we'll be stunned by the writers' freedom of expression: Some psalms are long and poetic, but others are shorter than a TV commercial. Some are prayers of joyful praise and gratitude, but others are miserable complaints — and many are both. Some prayers are directly connected to what the psalmists were experiencing, and other times the psalmists chose not to focus on their circumstances but instead looked to the transcendent. They talked to God about the past, and they talked to Him about the future, and they asked Him for strength and forgiveness and rescue and justice in the present.

Psalm 42:1 says, *"As a deer pants for flowing streams, so pants my soul for you, O God."* And here's the thing: Drinking water when we're thirsty doesn't feel like work. It isn't exhausting, inconvenient or stressful, and we don't need formal education or special skills to do it. Maybe prayer is the same way — it's not just something we're supposed to give *to* God but a way of receiving *from* Him everything we need. More than a continual challenge, prayer is a continual calling into deeper, sweeter, life-sustaining abiding with our heavenly Father.

What a relief!

We pray this study will be a blessing to you as we reflect on the psalms God has given us to guide our prayers — and we hope you'll also enjoy hearing from Proverbs 31 Ministries' Director of Theological Research, Dr. Joel Muddamalle, along the way as we learn, grow and pray together.

Welcome *to* Psalms.
— *Claire, Eric, Glynnis, Joel, Meghan, Michaela, Shae and Shelby*

WHAT IS PRAYER?

As we mentioned in the welcome letter to this study, God's Word tells us to *"pray without ceasing"* (1 Thessalonians 5:17). Some have taken this verse to mean we don't need to spend any specific time or even use words to pray; we simply pray all day as we think about God and what we need.

For instance, this idea is reflected in a poem by James Montgomery:

> Prayer is the soul's sincere desire,
> Unuttered or expressed;
> The motion of a hidden fire
> That trembles in the breast.
>
> Prayer is the burden of a sigh,
> The falling of a tear
> The upward glancing of an eye,
> When none but God is near.[1]

Certainly our upward glances may be counted as a beginning of prayer ... but prayer is also much more than that, according to God's Word. Sometimes our prayers may be simple expressions of emotions to God, but other times they may be more conversational. As we grow in our experience and confidence in prayer, we may even see our prayers change.

The simplest definition of prayer is "communication with God." But what does that look like? Many have sought to define prayer more specifically: Take, for example, these theological definitions:

- "Communication with God, primarily offered in the second-person voice (addressing God directly). May include petition, entreaty, supplication, thanksgiving, praise, hymns, and lament."[2]
- "Though prayer also includes adoration ... Christian prayer has always been essentially petitionary."[3]
- "The addressing and petitioning of God."[4]
- "The activity of bringing all our desires and thanksgiving to God with full humility and submission to his will, confident that God will hear and respond."[5]
- "Dialogue between God and people, especially His covenant partners."[6]

If some of these terms are difficult, don't worry! The point is how scholars vary in defining something so simple yet also very deep. This study is all about uncomplicating prayer — so we'll dig into what it means to do things like "petition" and "supplicate" (ways of presenting requests to God) as we study 30 psalms in the next six weeks. But for now, it's worth noting that all of these definitions share the idea that prayer is a form of communication from God's people to God Himself.

Many cultures and religions throughout history speak about communication with their gods — gods who sit in high, unreachable places, who must be begged and appeased to speak and be spoken to. But the God of the Bible, Yahweh, (Exodus 3:14) is unique in that He invites us to communicate with Him! Jesus said, *"If you ask me anything in my name, I will do it"* (John 14:14). He seems to love to listen. He says our prayers are like a pleasing aroma to Him. (Psalm 141:2; Revelation 5:8) And not only this — He speaks to us in His Word, and He shows us the very prayers He loves to answer! What an amazing God we have.

The variety of the psalms is beautiful because it speaks to the complexity of our lives. By noticing how the psalms reflect the full array of human emotion, we find the presence of a caring God who is not taken aback by honest expressions of feeling. Psalms can be broken up into a variety of genres, including:

- Praise.
- Confession.
- Thanksgiving .
- Lament (songs of sorrow).
- Trust (expressing trust in God or asking God to give the ability to trust).
- Wisdom (songs intended to teach us how life is to be lived as children of God).
- Intercession and supplication.

As we pray the psalms, we will find they reflect certain genres that will inform how we pray.

Why *Pray the* Psalms?

If prayer is communication with God, then all worship is prayer. Songs sung to God are also prayers. Poetry written to God is prayer. The biblical psalms, then, are all a form of prayer.

And this is the best part: Because the book of Psalms is part of God's very own Word, we can pray with confidence through the psalms as prayers of our own. If the psalms are God's Word, we know that when we pray them, we are praying God's own will. Why wouldn't He answer a prayer He Himself inspired? A prayer given to us by God implies a sure answer.

First John 5:14-15 says, *"And this is the confidence that we have toward him, that if we ask anything according to his will he hears us. And if we know that he hears us in whatever we ask, we know that we have the requests that we have asked of him."*

Praying the psalms not only gives us a massive amount of words to pray when we can't find words on our own, but it also gives us the faith to pray according to God's will. Then if God's answer is "no" for a specific request of ours, we can trust it is a "yes" for something better.

EXAMPLES OF PSALMS
LIKELY INFLUENCING
NEW TESTAMENT PRAYERS

In the following verses from Matthew, Mark, Luke, John and Acts, the prayers spoken by God's people so closely resemble the language of psalms that theologians suspect psalms were the inspiration. (Or in the case of Jesus, He was fulfilling psalms.) Spend a few moments comparing some of these verses:

NEW TESTAMENT PRAYER	SOME SHARED LANGUAGE/IDEAS	PSALMS
Matthew 11:25 (A prayer of Jesus)		Psalm 8:2
John 17:6; John 17:26 (A prayer of Jesus)		Psalm 22:22
John 17:12 (A prayer of Jesus)		Psalm 109:8
Luke 23:46 (A prayer of Jesus)		Psalm 31:5
Matthew 6:10 (A prayer of Jesus)		Psalm 103:21
Matthew 27:46 (A prayer of Jesus)		Psalm 22:1

Luke 1:46-55 (Mary's Song)		Psalm 34:2-3,10; Psalm 35:9; Psalm 69:30; Psalm 71:19; Psalm 72:17; Psalm 75:7; Psalm 89:1-2, 8, 10
Acts 4:23-31 (A prayer of Peter and John)		Psalm 2:1-2; Psalm 102:25; Psalm 124:8; Psalm 134:3; Psalm 138:7; Psalm 146:6
Acts 7:59 (A prayer of Stephen)		Psalm 31:5

NOTE FROM JOEL

The focus of our study is Psalms, but one of the things we want to do is see how all of Scripture is interconnected through divine design. In other words, the divine author (God) provided intentional direction for the Scriptures we have today.

I find it fascinating that the psalmists, under God's inspiration, were students of their own tradition: For instance, the psalms that may have been the inspiration for Mary's song in Luke 1:46-55 were likely inspired first by Hannah's song of praise in 1 Samuel 2. We can then connect Hannah's song of praise all the way back to what many Old Testament scholars believe is the first ancient song of the people of Israel: the "Song of the Sea" in Exodus 15 that recounts the faithfulness of God as He led the Israelites into safety and security.

All of Scripture is connected. The psalms evidence the rich story of God's people and therefore are an invitation for us to participate in that story as the people of God today.

How To Build a

HABIT OF PRAYER

Knowing that God wants us to communicate with Him, we might ask: When? Where? How do we build a habit of prayer?

The Bible gives us a lot of freedom in answering that question, but it's clear God wants us to pray. God didn't create prayer as a chore we *have* to do, feeling guilty when we fail; it's an active conversation He invites us to join. Prayer is something we *get* to do as believers in Christ.

WHERE DO WE FIND MOTIVATION AND POWER TO PRAY?

What we do in Christ can be called good work, or fruit, and this is a result of the Holy Spirit living in us. (Galatians 5:22-24) Where there is no Spirit, there is no fruit of the Spirit. First Corinthians 2:14 says, *"The natural person does not accept the things of the Spirit of God, for they are folly to him, and he is not able to understand them because they are spiritually discerned."* Before knowing Christ, all of us had our minds set not on spiritual things but on worldly things. But when we trust in Jesus, *"the Spirit of God dwells in [us]"* (Romans 8:9). The Spirit then spurs us on to spiritual disciplines, including prayer. He is our source of motivation and power.

So the beginning of a habit of prayer is to know and love the God we are praying to.

Thank God! The beginning of prayer is faith and love for Christ. God's Word teaches that we would have no access to God if it weren't for the work of Christ. This is why God's Word says to us in Ephesians 2:12, *"Remember that you were at [one] time separated from Christ ... having no hope and without God in the world."* But Jesus paid the price on the cross for us and granted us the access we now have to address God. He is our mediator. He is our go-between. (1 Timothy 2:5-6) This is why Christians pray in Jesus' name. (John 14:14) Jesus is how our prayers reach God.

Knowing Jesus is the foundation of prayer that is powerful and effective. James 5:16b says, *"The prayer of a **righteous** person has great power as it is working"* (emphasis added). And as believers in Christ, we have been made righteous by His blood! (2 Corinthians 5:21)

This really great news causes our hearts to overflow with love toward the One who saved us from our sin. And nobody has to force us to talk to someone we love, right? We long to talk with those we love. So to increase our habit of prayer is to increase our love for the Lord.

HOW DO WE LEARN TO LOVE GOD MORE SO THAT WE PRAY MORE?

Here's one way: Jesus said, *"he who is forgiven little, loves little"* (Luke 7:47b). This also implies that he or she who is forgiven much, loves much. If we know we are wicked, broken sinners saved by God's grace alone and not by anything good in ourselves, then we know God's amazing love for us — and in return, we love Him all the more.

David, the man God used to record most of the prayers in the book of Psalms, was well acquainted with his own wickedness and the forgiveness he received from God. After Nathan confronted David for adultery and murder, although there would be significant consequences, *"David said to Nathan, 'I have sinned against the LORD.' And Nathan said to David, 'The LORD also has put away your sin; you shall not die"* (2 Samuel 12:13). This was tremendous grace, especially since this happened during a time when Israel was governed by the old covenant of the law.

To understand the depth of our sin, we also study God's law. We read the Ten Commandments in Exodus 20. We study His holiness. Like a mirror, God's law shows us how utterly short we fall of being worthy of eternal life. (Isaiah 6:5) But if we reject our life of rebellion and turn to Him, He runs to us with open arms and receives us as His children just like the father received his prodigal son in Luke 15:11-32.

Then, motivated by His love, we desire to thank our Savior by obeying Him and imitating Him. It's at that point we can receive examples from Jesus Himself and rise early in the morning to pray. We can take joy in fasting and praying like Jesus did in the wilderness. (Matthew 4:1-4) We can pray into the night like He did in the garden of Gethsemane. (Matthew 26:36-46) We can also do as God's servants did in the Old Testament: David prayed at seven different times throughout the day. (Psalm 119:164) Daniel prayed three times a day. (Daniel 6:10) But the point is not the number of prayers — it's the passion for God that fuels them.

WHAT DOES THIS MEAN FOR TODAY? WHERE DO WE START?

Some days we have less time to pray than others. But perhaps somewhat ironically, praying may be a way to increase the time you have to pray! Church reformer Martin Luther was known to have said, "I have so much to do today that I shall spend the first three hours in prayer."[1] However and whenever we pray, it seems clear from Scripture that we are called to pray frequently.

God also wants us to use words when we pray. When our Lord Jesus said, *"pray then like this"* (Matthew 6:9), what followed were words. And Jesus' mention of *"our daily bread"* in the Lord's Prayer (Matthew 6:11) implies at least daily prayer.

Maybe you haven't prayed daily in a long time — or ever — and if so, you're not alone! We're in this together. You can start today, right where you are: The Lord's Prayer in Matthew 6, just four sentences long, shows us that God is honored by even a short prayer. (To learn more about this, flip to "Praying the Lord's Prayer" on page 130.)

Or maybe you struggle with wanting to pray regularly because you know God is in control and does all He pleases. (Psalm 115:3) It may help to remember that throughout Scripture, God is pleased to work and act after prayer (e.g., 2 Chronicles 33:12-13; Numbers 14:13-20; Mark 9:25-29; Acts 9:40-41). Answers to prayers happen after prayers. So in the very act of praying, we are writing a part of the history of how God loves to move, act and answer. It pleases God for it to be so.

We hope the rest of this study guide will help you continue to build a habit of daily praying *"on all occasions with all kinds of prayers and requests"* (Ephesians 6:18, NIV). In the years to come, we pray you'll look back and see how God has strengthened you so that you might ***"in everything*** *by prayer and supplication with thanksgiving let your requests be made known to God"* (Philippians 4:6, emphasis added).

Some may wonder why we should focus specifically on words. I love what my friend and fellow *Therapy & Theology* co-host, therapist Jim Cress, says: "Our words frame our reality." Getting into the habit of verbally relating and communicating with God is a practice of reinforcing truths about God and who we are in light of God. To say that our words frame our reality is to acknowledge that what comes out of our mouths usually indicates what is present deep within our hearts. Making a commitment to use words in our prayers is multifaceted: First, we learn from Scripture what words to use. Second, we can consider the words that flow out of our mouths to help us consider the condition of our hearts. We may find that the honest words we pray will actually teach us about what we need to pray for.

Fun Facts About
PRAYER & THE PSALMS

- The book of Psalms is divided into 150 chapters, which contain a total of roughly 2,500 verses.

- Many scholars believe there are five "books" or sections within the psalms. Part of their reasoning is that Psalms 1, 42, 73, 90 and 107 start with a doxology — a praise to God for His Word or His goodness — each introducing a new section in the book.

- Psalms has more named authors than any other book of the Bible. These include: David, the sons of Korah, Moses, Asaph, Solomon, Heman the Ezrahite and Ethan the Ezrahite. Additionally, many psalms are anonymous.

- Five psalms are actually titled "A Prayer": Psalms 17, 86, 90, 102 and 142.

- While all the psalms can be considered prayer, the most common Hebrew noun meaning "prayer," תְּפִלָּה (*te.phil.lah*), is only used 29 times. In the ESV translation, Hebrew words meaning "to ask" and "please!" are also translated "pray" in some cases. If you have a smartphone, you can scan this  QR code and see a list of the uses of תְּפִלָּה / "prayer" in the psalms. (Otherwise you will need to type this address into a browser: https://www.stepbible.org/?q=version=ESV|reference=Ps|strong=H8605&options=NHVUG)[1]

What You Have To *Look Forward* to in This Study

DAILY TEACHINGS AND REFLECTION QUESTIONS

Each week of this study includes daily teachings on five biblical psalms. We'll process each psalm together and think about how it can help us uncomplicate our prayer lives today. You'll also find daily questions to guide your personal study.

PSALM ANNOTATION EXERCISES

For our fifth day of study each week, we'll include the full text of one psalm and invite you to take notes and mark up the text alongside us as we look at the words and images of the Scriptures in depth. Then we'll use the psalm to pray God's Word back to Him.

WEEKEND REFLECTION AND PRAYER

Each weekend, we'll summarize some important ideas we've learned throughout the week and close with a prayer.

BONUS CONTENT

Sprinkled throughout this guide, you'll also find some special insights and notes from theology expert Dr. Joel Muddamalle! Occasionally we'll also dive into a Hebrew word study, explore the relationship between prayer and our emotions, learn about how Jesus prays for us, and more.

PRAYING THE LORD'S PRAYER

At the end of our study, we've included an additional resource you can use to pray like Jesus did in Matthew 6, using the Lord's Prayer to shape your own conversations with God.

TABLE OF CONTENTS

WEEK 4
Prayers of
Lament

DAY 16 *(Psalm 102)*
For the woman who needs to say she's not OK.

DAY 17 *(Psalm 10)*
For the woman who doesn't know how to pray when it seems like evil is winning.

DAY 18 *(Psalm 90)*
For the woman who needs a way to grieve with hope.

DAY 19 *(Psalm 22)*
For the woman who needs to know she's not alone.

DAY 20 *(Psalm 142)*
For the woman who is desperate for a safe place.

WEEK 5
Prayers of
Supplication

DAY 21 *(Psalm 37)*
For the woman who needs to be reminded she can talk to God about anything.

DAY 22 *(Psalm 17)*
For the woman who longs to be delivered out of the hardship she's facing.

DAY 23 *(Psalm 143)*
For the woman who is asking God, *What's next? Where do I go from here?*

DAY 24 *(Psalm 31)*
For the woman who is continuing to pray even when her circumstances haven't changed.

DAY 25 *(Psalm 121)*
For the woman who is placing her hope in the helping hands of God.

WEEK 6
Prayers of
Intercession

DAY 26 *(Psalm 106)*
For the woman who needs the reminder that redemption is always possible.

DAY 27 *(Psalm 60)*
For the woman who needs God to do what she can't do for the people she loves.

DAY 28 *(Psalm 20)*
For the woman whose loved ones are facing a battle.

DAY 29 *(Psalm 28)*
For the woman who needs confidence that the Lord will carry her and her people.

DAY 30 *(Psalm 33)*
For the woman who wants to celebrate what God has done in her and her loved ones' lives.

ascribe/

worship/

his holy name/

praise/

extol/

king of glory/

who he is/

As we begin our prayer journey through the book of Psalms, it's right, but maybe not entirely natural, that we start with prayers of adoration or praise.

When we start to pray, it's so easy to move quickly to thanksgiving or requests — depending on the day and what we've been through. And sometimes a quick "emergency prayer" is all we can manage. But the psalmists invite us to back up a bit and pause ... take a breath ... and focus on the One we love and serve.

Adoring God is different than being thankful for Him. Adoration is praise that originates from our hearts and that we pour out on God. It's a declaration and elevation of His character and acts. Thanksgiving is our response to the love, blessing and compassion that flows from God onto us.

When we pause to praise God in prayer, it repositions our hearts. And as we refocus on who God is, we are reminded that no matter what we face today, God is bigger than our circumstances. Praise magnifies God to the position He deserves in our lives, and our problems diminish in light of His majesty.

So today we'll look at Psalm 145, the only biblical psalm actually subtitled "A Song of Praise." In fact, Psalms 145-150 have been called the "grand doxology of the entire collection" of psalms, as these six psalms focus on praise.[1]

Psalm 145:3 clearly and simply declares why praise is important: *"Great is the LORD, and greatly to be praised, and his greatness is unsearchable."*

Prayers of adoration are easier to pray when we know more about God's greatness. Psalm 145 demonstrates that the psalmist, King David, *"a man after [God's] own heart"* (1 Samuel 13:14), knew God intimately. But even if we haven't experienced God in all the ways described in this psalm, we can learn about Him through others' praises. That's why the psalms are so helpful as we learn how to pray.

In verses 4-7, we see that God's people passed down testimonies of His actions through the generations. These faithful actions are reasons to praise God.

How does David describe God's actions in verses 4-7?

These verses speak of a God who acts, and what He *does* always perfectly reflects who He *is*. He is not an absent God. He is not disconnected from His people. He *is* observant and engaged.

> In what ways has God acted on your behalf or your family's behalf?

As we work through this study, we will see the power of praying God's words back to Him, as King David demonstrates in verse 8. This verse includes one of the most-quoted sayings in the Old Testament, first spoken by God to Moses on Mount Sinai as God was preparing the second set of tablets containing the Ten Commandments. (Exodus 34:6) These special words weren't just ascribed to God by humans; God declared this about *Himself*.

> Write Psalm 145:8 below and circle the descriptors of God that most stand out to you as worthy of adoration. Of these characteristics, which ones do you most need to experience today? Why?

Starting with Psalm 145:14, we find a series of beautiful descriptions of a caring heavenly Father attuned to the needs of His children. As we look more closely at who God helps, we see His compassion toward those who are hurting, fallen, needy and afraid.

If that's you today, take comfort in knowing your Father sees you and knows what you need. And as we have learned today, He is a God who acts on His children's behalf.

Describe God's character in your own words from what you read in verses 14-20.

A PRAYER FOR YOU:

Lord, You are great and "greatly to be praised" *(Psalm 145:3). I will remember all the ways You have worked in my life and testify of Your goodness to all. I will tell of the ways I've seen You act in the lives of those around me. I'm so grateful You are gracious and merciful, and I want to worship You more for who You are today, tomorrow and always. In Jesus' name, amen.*

We can almost picture a darkened hillside with King David resting on the ground, looking up at the sky, as he wrote Psalm 8 ... the immensity of God's glory and the comparative smallness of humanity brightly illuminated before him.

This psalm is a celebration of awe and wonder, two appropriate responses when we experience the reality of who God is. And adding to the amazement, this same God who is over all creation actually thinks about us!

What a reassuring truth this is for all who feel unseen and overlooked by the artificial light of our world that seems to shine most brightly on a few. Here in Psalm 8, we are all invited to worship the One who created light and created us. (vv. 3-5) And we find some patterns of praise we can use in our own prayers.

The opening of this psalm expresses the multifaceted relationship we have with God. In verse 1, David first addressed God using His personal name, translated in English as *"Lord"* in all caps. We see intimacy in this use of God's name, which God first gave Moses in Exodus 3 when He revealed Himself in a burning bush.

Then David addressed God with what looks to be the same word in English ("Lord") but is translated from a different Hebrew word, *adonai*, meaning "master." Here we see David acknowledge God's dominion and power over all of creation.

> We are all invited to approach God and know Him intimately yet also know Him as Lord over all. Do you find it more comfortable to interact with God as a close friend or as a ruler and leader? Why?

> How has your relationship with the Lord affected your ability to praise Him in prayer?

The size of the universe is incomprehensible. Science makes educated guesses, but according to NASA, the visible universe would take 15 billion light-years to cross.[1] And according to Psalm 8, the same God who made all that is mindful of us!

"What is man that you are mindful of him, and the son of man that you care for him?" (Psalm 8:4)

Saying God is *"mindful of [us]"* means we are more than just a passing thought to Him. In other places in Scripture, God remembers His people by acknowledging His promise to them and enacting rescue or help.

Read the following verses and note what you learn about God's remembrance of His people:

GENESIS 8:1

GENESIS 30:22

EXODUS 2:24

ACTS 10:30-31

According to theologian Derek Kidner, "Mindful has a compassionately purposeful ring, since God's remembering always implies his movement toward the object of his memory ..."[2]

What do you learn about God's character by knowing you are on His mind?

As we wrap up today's study, let's look at verse 5, where the psalmist continues to be in awe of God's creation of humanity: *"You have made him a little lower than the heavenly beings and crowned him with glory and honor."*

If we look to Hebrews 2:9, we see this verse applied to Jesus, *"who for a little while was made lower than the angels"* when He lived on earth but is now *"crowned with glory and honor because of the suffering of death, so that by the grace of God he might taste death for everyone."*

Jesus is our best reason to praise God. It is only through His death and resurrection and our faith in Him that we can enter into God's presence at all.

Take some time to praise God for how He has perfectly revealed His image and character in His Son, Jesus. (Colossians 1:15) List a few things you adore about Him:

A PRAYER FOR YOU:

Lord, I am amazed that You created the heavens and the earth, including all that is in it. You are sovereign over all, yet You still remember me. There is no one like You. You alone are God and worthy to be praised. I pause in my day today to recognize how much I need You because on my own I am powerless. Thank You for being my God and caring for me. In Jesus' name, amen.

When our back is against the wall, and the battle we face feels unwinnable ...
When there's not enough in the bank to cover a bill ...
When a relationship is dissolving or our health is at risk ...

These are the times we need God to show up in a big way, and our requests can tumble out in a rapid-fire to-do list.

There's nothing wrong with asking God for help. It shows our faithful trust in Him to act on our behalf. But what if we praised God for what He is able to do rather than just asking Him to do it? In light of that, we read Psalm 46 today, which gives us words to pray as a battle cry to the One who wins every battle He chooses to fight.

In Psalm 46, the psalmists, the sons of Korah, start by declaring God's power over trouble. We don't know if they were facing something urgent at the moment, but it's interesting that they didn't make any requests of God. We see direct requests in other psalms, but in this one, rather than start with the problem, the psalmists started with the provision: God Himself.

The psalmists may have been desperate for help, but rather than dissolve into fear, they boldly stated exactly what God is able to do. They declared the Truth of God's character and power in a way that stirred their faith. And we can use this same pattern of praise to stir our faith and prepare our hearts for whatever we face.

What are you facing today, or have you faced in the past, that is/was overwhelming?

What attributes of God would bring you peace today as you face that challenge? Use Psalm 46 as a guide.

The confidence of the psalmists is striking in Psalm 46. They imagined the very worst physical catastrophe, if the earth gave way and the sea roared, (vv. 2-3) but calmly testified that even then, we wouldn't need to fear because God would be there.

Isn't this confidence amazing? We can be sure the psalmists' confidence was neither self-generated nor tethered to their ability to save themselves. That would feel very insecure indeed and could lead to fear.

The promise found in Psalm 46 is that in the midst of our deepest fear — in the most tremendous disaster we may face — the Lord of Hosts is with us. The phrase *"LORD of hosts"* (v. 7) is a militaristic Hebrew phrase and speaks to God as the King of the heavenly army. But there is a huge difference between the type of King our God is and the kings of the world. In war, the kings and leaders of the world often stay back in hiding and safety and security. They wield strength, power and control from a position far behind the armies they send into battle. In Psalm 46, God is the type of King who is on the front line of battle. He alone wields ultimate strength; the King is in total control, and all power flows out from Him. In the midst of our fear, the promise of Psalm 46 is the presence of the King who leads us personally through our pain.[1]

When fear takes over, it's often a sign we are trusting someone or something other than God for help and strength. We trust our jobs for provision or the weather for our safety. But only God is completely dependable. Identify at least one fear you have and what/whom you are trusting other than God.

The psalmists praised God with a God-given confidence. This is surely the soul-rest Jesus spoke about in Matthew 11:28-29 when He said: *"Come to me, all who labor and are heavy laden, and I will give you rest. Take my yoke upon you, and learn from me, for I am gentle and lowly in heart, and you will find rest for your souls."*

The only way we will experience this rest for our souls is when our souls rest in God. Psalm 46 invites us to rest in the knowledge that God is in control and shows us how to affirm God's power in prayer. God will show up in times of trouble. The question is: Do we believe it?

Let's end today's study by writing declarations about God and why we can trust Him based on Psalm 46. For example: God is our <u>fortress</u>.

GOD IS _____.

GOD IS _____.

GOD IS _____.

GOD IS _____.

A PRAYER FOR YOU:

Lord, You are my refuge and strength. Before I have a need, You have already provided a solution. No matter what I face today, You have all resources at Your command. Although I believe that with my head, sometimes my heart doubts Your willingness to act on my behalf. Help my faith to grow as I meditate on who You truly are and Your love for me. In Jesus' name, amen.

Have you ever attended a concert or sporting event where the crowd roared with joy at the performance? People jump to their feet with shouts of approval. How exciting it is to celebrate the talent, excellence, hard work and success of someone we adore. It becomes transcendent, even, as for a moment all cares slip from thought.

How much more joyful should our celebration be in the presence of our heavenly Father, whose majesty and excellence are unmarred by the human frailty or inconsistency of those we follow on the stage or field?

The psalmist who wrote Psalm 95 knew this joy in the Lord, and his psalm invites us into such a celebration.

Psalm 95 has two distinct parts. The first is an exuberant invitation to come into the presence of God.

> Read Psalm 95:1-6 and list the activities we are called to participate in when we enter God's presence.

This approach to worship isn't subdued and spiritless. In fact, though it might feel a bit uncomfortable or maybe irreverent to make *"joyful noise"* (vv. 1-2), the psalmist set aside any thoughts of himself or his circumstances to celebrate the One he served.

We see a similar abandon when King David celebrated the return of the Ark of the Covenant in 2 Samuel 6. David's joy was uncontainable as he danced before the people.

> Read 2 Samuel 6:16-22. What reason did David give for his celebration in verse 21? Can you identify similar reasons for you to rejoice in prayer?

It can be hard to praise God when our circumstances don't feel joyful. Yet we are called throughout Scripture to exercise and practice joy. Philippians 4:4 is one well-known verse, where Paul exhorts us to *"rejoice in the Lord always."*

> List the reasons we can rejoice at all times, according to Psalm 95. How can focusing on God's attributes help us find true joy in His presence?

Starting at verse 8, the celebration shifts to a warning. While this may seem odd, it might help us to remember the psalms were created for public worship. Scholars believe Psalm 95 might have been prepared for the Feast of Tabernacles, "when God's people re-lived, in token, their time of encampment in the wilderness."[1]

Although the people had seen God's powerful miracles, they still doubted and questioned God. For example, the psalmist mentions Meribah, where the Israelites grumbled. (Numbers 20:2-13) The Hebrews' wanderings could be summed up in one word: unbelief. This unbelief displeased God, and He refused entrance into the promised land to the first generation of Israelites He delivered from Egypt. (Numbers 14)

> God welcomes our honest questions in prayer. But there is a type of questioning that offends God. What warning can we gain from Psalm 95:8-11 about the wrong way to question God? How does cultivating praise in our prayers help keep our hearts right?

Let's end with a hopeful promise found in Hebrews 3:7-4:13, which references Psalm 95:8-11. The Israelites' unbelief kept them from entering the promised land and receiving God's rest, but today there is beautiful hope for those united by faith in Jesus. We still have the opportunity to experience God's Sabbath rest. (Hebrews 4:9-10) Scholar Donald Guthrie puts it this way: "What believers can now enter is none other than the same kind of rest which the Creator enjoyed when he had completed his works, which means that the rest idea is of completion and not of inactivity."[2]

What an incredible gift. We not only have the peace that comes from the completion of our work but the peace that comes from the completed work Jesus did on the cross for our salvation. When we trust that God has completed all that needs to be done, we can truly rejoice!

A PRAYER FOR YOU:

Almighty Lord, You are joy, and in You, I can find joy that is separated from my circumstances. I am amazed You have the power to redirect my mind and heart away from problems and give me peace. When I lift my eyes to You, I am reminded nothing is outside of Your control. You are the Good Shepherd who always cares for His sheep. I put my trust in You because only You are fully trustworthy. In Jesus' name, amen.

DOES GOD NEED OUR PRAISE?

As we reflect on the importance of adoration and why we should heed David's urging to *"sing to the LORD"* (Psalm 95:1), we might find ourselves wondering ...

Does God really need to hear me tell Him how amazing He is all the time?

The short answer is: No. In fact, if the Lord needed our praises to validate Him, He would not be the Lord. Our triune God — Father, Son and Spirit — is perfectly fulfilled and perfectly adored in and of Himself. He needs nothing; He has everything. (Acts 17:24-25)

So praising God is fundamentally different from other kinds of praise we might be familiar with. We praise our children, for example, to encourage them when they do well on a test they studied hard for; otherwise, they may feel their efforts are unimportant. But God is never in danger of insecurity. We can't add to His importance — we can only recognize the supreme importance He already possesses. (Revelation 4:8; Revelation 21:6)

In other words: **We praise God simply because He is infinitely praiseworthy. God doesn't *need* our prayers of adoration, but He *deserves* and *desires* them.** When Scripture tells us *"the Father is seeking ... people to worship him"* (John 4:23), this doesn't mean God is recruiting cheerleaders. He is inviting us to rightly see and know Him as Lord, and when we do that, praise is the inevitable result! As we tell God how amazing He is, we also remind ourselves that we are amazingly loved by Him — so God is pleased to receive the adoration He is due, and we are blessed and fulfilled by adoring Him.

DAY 5 · PSALM 40
For the woman who needs a revelation of who God really is.

We close our week together by looking at Psalm 40, which is often considered a thanksgiving psalm and was written by King David. In addition to thanksgiving, we also see elements of praise and petition. Even though this isn't designated as a "psalm of adoration" by theologians, every part of the Bible, including Psalm 40, reveals who God is.

Our exercise today is to read through Psalm 40 and underline or highlight words or phrases that tell us something about God's character. Then, to the right of the psalm, identify the characteristics of God and note why He is worthy of praise. (We've completed verse 1 for you as an example below.)

As you make your list, you'll find so many reasons to praise God for who He is to you.

PSALM 40
MY HELP AND MY DELIVERER
To the choirmaster. A Psalm of David.

NOTES

¹ *I waited patiently for the LORD;*
   he inclined to me and heard my cry.
² *He drew me up from the pit of destruction,*
   out of the miry bog,
and set my feet upon a rock,
   making my steps secure.
³ *He put a new song in my mouth,*
   a song of praise to our God.
Many will see and fear,
   and put their trust in the LORD.

V. 1 — God listens to His children and draws near to us. He isn't aloof but is compassionate and caring.

NOTE FROM JOEL

In this psalm, we see the character of God, and the action of God is consistent with His character. First, there is a petition from the psalmist: In verse 1, there is a cry from the child of God. But then notice God's three actions after He hears the cry of His child:
1. He draws us up.
2. He sets our feet.
3. He puts a new song in our mouth.

These actions of God provide three comforts for us:
1. We are brought high, a phrase that speaks of honor bestowed upon us.
2. He grants us the stability we long for. When things are out of control, we find stability in the One who holds all things together.
3. We sing because we've experienced the goodness of God.

⁴ Blessed is the man who makes
*the L*ORD *his trust,*
who does not turn to the proud,
to those who go astray after a lie!
*⁵ You have multiplied, O L*ORD *my God,*
your wondrous deeds and your thoughts toward us;
none can compare with you!
I will proclaim and tell of them,
yet they are more than can be told.

⁶ In sacrifice and offering you have not delighted,
but you have given me an open ear.
Burnt offering and sin offering
you have not required.
⁷ Then I said, "Behold, I have come;
in the scroll of the book it is written of me:
⁸ I delight to do your will, O my God;
your law is within my heart."

⁹ I have told the glad news of deliverance
in the great congregation;
behold, I have not restrained my lips,
*as you know, O L*ORD.
¹⁰ I have not hidden your deliverance within my heart;
I have spoken of your faithfulness and your salvation;
I have not concealed your steadfast love and your
faithfulness
from the great congregation.

*¹¹ As for you, O L*ORD, *you will not restrain*
your mercy from me;
your steadfast love and your faithfulness will
ever preserve me!
¹² For evils have encompassed me
beyond number;
my iniquities have overtaken me,
and I cannot see;
they are more than the hairs of my head;
my heart fails me.

¹³ Be pleased, O LORD, to deliver me!
O LORD, make haste to help me!
¹⁴ Let those be put to shame and disappointed altogether
who seek to snatch away my life;
let those be turned back and brought to dishonor
who delight in my hurt!
¹⁵ Let those be appalled because of their shame
who say to me, "Aha, Aha!"

¹⁶ But may all who seek you
rejoice and be glad in you;
may those who love your salvation
say continually, "Great is the LORD!"
¹⁷ As for me, I am poor and needy,
but the Lord takes thought for me.
You are my help and my deliverer;
do not delay, O my God!

REFLECTION QUESTIONS:

1. David begins this psalm by remembering God's faithfulness. What happens in our relationship with God when we do the same?
2. David is honest about his failures and vulnerable enough to share them with others. What must David have believed about God to move him to such honesty?
3. In the next few days, who is one person you could tell about God's faithfulness to you?

YOUR PRAYER:

To complete the week, write a prayer of adoration including some of what you've learned about God.

NOTES

NOTES

NOTES

Week 1

WEEKEND REFLECTION

As we come to the end of our first week of this study, it's good to remind ourselves why we started a study of prayer and psalms with the concept of adoration or praise. To answer that question, let's move to the New Testament book of Matthew, where religious leaders asked Jesus a question: *"Teacher, which is the great commandment in the Law?"* (Matthew 22:36).

Jesus' answer helps us understand why it's important to cultivate praise into our prayers: *"You shall love the Lord your God with all your heart and with all your soul and with all your mind. This is the great and first commandment"* (Matthew 22:37-38).

Prayers of adoration help us grow in our love and affection for God — not just for what He can do for us but for who He is. If we wanted to show intentional love to a friend or a family member, we probably wouldn't first present a list of requests or ask their forgiveness. Those things might happen, but we'd start with a declaration of love, possibly including specific examples of what we love about them.

The same idea can be applied to God but in greater measure.

One day, every creature on earth and in heaven will praise God. Every knee will bow in reverence to Him. Creating a habit of praise in your prayers will open your eyes to what heaven already knows: He is worthy!

"And I heard every creature in heaven and on earth and under the earth and in the sea, and all that is in them, saying, 'To him who sits on the throne and to the Lamb be blessing and honor and glory and might forever and ever!'" (Revelation 5:13)

A PRAYER FOR YOU:

Great are You, Lord! You are my help and my deliverer. You hear Your children's prayers, and You know when we are in despair. I praise You for Your perfect compassion that moves You to act for my good. Your goodness has never failed; You've never abandoned a promise. I'm so grateful that You think of me and love me. In Jesus' name, amen.

forgive/

onfess/

ins/

orry /

niquity /

pardon /

guilt/

We aren't exactly born with a desire to admit our mistakes. If you've ever spent time with toddlers, you know they don't willingly admit when they have been disobedient. We are born with a bent to sin and to cover it up when we do.

Can we ever change?

This week, we will shift our focus to prayers of confession. Now, before you close this book and walk away because that sounds too hard, let's get a different perspective. By definition, confession is an act of faith. First John 1:9 says we confess our sins because God *"is faithful and just to forgive us our sins and to cleanse us from all unrighteousness."* And a profession of faith is also a kind of confession: Romans 10:9 says, *"if you confess with your mouth that Jesus is Lord and believe in your heart that God raised him from the dead, you will be saved."* This is a requisite for salvation!

What is your current understanding of confession? How does it make you feel?

In Scripture, "confession" often refers to acknowledgement of our sins before God — and in some cases also before a fellow Christ follower or anyone we have sinned against.

Read Leviticus 16:21 in the Old Testament and James 5:16 in the New Testament. The key word in both is "confess." But what differences do you notice?

In the Old Testament, animal sacrifice was required for confession on a special Day of Atonement. Today, because of the sacrifice of Christ, we can confess our sins to God and one another without an elaborate ceremony. Thank God! Admitting what we've done wrong, the things we aren't proud of, and the moments that make us want to hide in shame doesn't sound like the access code to change. **But acknowledging our faults and failures paves the way for us to experience freedom.**

David, the author of today's psalm, brought his sins before God. While we don't know the circumstances he faced, we do know that in asking God to save him, he admitted he was not innocent.

> How many times does David use the words *"sin," "transgression," "guilt," "trouble," "afflict"* or *"shame"* in Psalm 25?

The thought of having to wait on what God *will do* can be very frustrating. The most important people never have to wait; they have VIP or "all access" passes to everything. But Psalm 25:3 gives us a countercultural direction when it comes to our relationship with God: We are called to wait on Him and know that our patience will not result in shame. Old Testament scholar James Hamilton says, "Waiting for Yahweh is a strategy for fighting sin and a posture of confidence against enemies."[1] For the believer, waiting is not an act of weakness but a display of confident strength.

David's confession of his sins didn't leave him in despair and dismay; it reminded him of his desperate need for God. He knew God was the only One who could rescue him.

David does three things in his confession that we can also practice:

1. REFERENCE GOD'S CHARACTER. Throughout this psalm, David stated characteristics of God. His love is steadfast, (v. 10) He is good, (v. 8) He does not put us to shame, (v. 3) and He pardons our guilt. (v. 11)

> What other characteristics of God does David mention in his prayer? Write some here, and highlight some in your Bible too.

2. REMEMBER WHAT HE HAS DONE. Knowing that God instructed and brought His people out of their distress in the past (*"from of old"*) gives us hope that we, too, can move forward after we sin (vv. 6-7).

3. REMIND OURSELVES OF WHAT GOD *WILL* DO BECAUSE OF WHO HE IS. In referencing God's characteristics, David reminded himself that God would forgive him, instruct him and deliver him from trouble. (vv. 3, 8, 15)

Friend, change is possible. Confession is the first step in admitting that we can't do it on our own and that only God can save us.

What patterns or behaviors in your life feel impossible to overcome? What does Luke 1:37 say about what is impossible for God?

Confession is not about shaming us — it's about freeing us from the weight of shame. **When we stop hiding, we can start healing.**

Read Romans 8:1 and fill in the blanks:

"THERE IS THEREFORE NOW NO _____ FOR

THOSE WHO ARE IN _____ _____."

A PRAYER FOR YOU:

To end our day of studying Psalm 25, write a prayer, like David did, for the Lord to teach you His path (v. 4) as you practice confession today.

One of the most beautiful parts of confession is getting to experience forgiveness. Whether we receive forgiveness from another person or especially from God, there is a joy that comes from being forgiven.

> Read Isaiah 1:18 and Micah 7:19. How does it make you feel to know the result of confession is God's forgiveness?

When we are in Christ, nothing we do can outweigh His love for us. Over and over again, He is faithful and just to forgive us when we sin. This is good news!

In today's psalm, Psalm 32, there are four Hebrew terms used for "sin." Each of them highlights different aspects of sin:

1. *Pesha'* (vv. 1, 5, translated *"transgression"*) denotes the basic idea of rebellion.
2. *Hata'ah* (v. 1, translated *"sin"*) is a more general term referring to a deliberate offense.
3. *'Awon* (vv. 2, 5, translated *"iniquity"*) implies crime and going astray.
4. *Remiyyah* (v. 2, translated *"deceit"*) emphasizes falsehood or even hypocrisy.

> Which of these aspects of sin do you think is easiest for you to recognize in yourself? Which one is easier to miss?

There are also three different Hebrew verbs in Psalm 32 that function as mirror opposites of *Pesha'* (transgression), *Hata'ah* (sin) and *'Awon* (iniquity), showing three aspects of forgiveness: 1) to be unburdened, 2) to have an offense covered, and 3) to be legally acquitted.

> Reread Psalm 32:6-7. What happens when we offer prayers of confession? What did David say God was for him?

When we confess in prayer, not only do we **find God**, but He also **hides us** from the eternal consequences of our sin. We may read about the joy of the *"upright"* (v. 11) and feel unworthy of this — but when Jesus rose from the grave, He made a way for us to receive *His* uprightness. That means in Christ, we are lifted out of our sin. We are covered. We aren't liable for punishment. It's not confession that saves us. It's Jesus who saves us. (John 1:29)

Lastly, in your Bible, you may have noticed this psalm is called "A Maskil of David." A *maskil* was a song of wisdom, written either to be sung or easily recited. There is wisdom in confession.

Reread Psalm 32:3-4. What happens to us when we unwisely avoid confession?

The problem is that because we are sinful, we don't want to admit we sin! But thankfully, God gave us the Holy Spirit, who convicts us. (John 16:8) Only by His power do we experience heart change.

In Psalm 32:1-2, what happens to those who are forgiven?

The forgiven are blessed! So let's practice confession by praying like David in Psalm 32.

A PRAYER FOR YOU:

Father, Your Word says the one whose transgression is forgiven and whose sin is covered is blessed. (Psalm 32:1) Let there be no iniquity or deceit in me. (v. 2) When I am silent in my sin, I waste away. But when I acknowledge it and don't cover it up, You forgive me. (vv. 3-5) So I confess my sins before You now and turn away from them. Thank You for being my hiding place, preserving me from my trouble, and surrounding me with shouts of deliverance. (v. 7) Teach me. Counsel me. Surround me with Your steadfast love because I trust in You. I will be glad and shout for joy! (vv. 9-11) In Jesus' name, amen.

When we mess up, it can feel hard to come to God. Whether it's because we feel ashamed or because we don't know how to fix what's been done, approaching God after we have sinned can be the last thing we want to do. But the reality is: Confessing is the best thing we can do so nothing is standing between us and God.

Describe a moment in your life when you felt like something was blocking you from God. What was the blockage?

Psalm 38 is subtitled *"for the memorial offering."* Some translations may say *"to bring remembrance"* (CSB). Throughout Scripture, requesting that God remember something was another way of asking Him to act in a situation.[1]

Take a few minutes to write down some words and phrases David used to describe how he felt in this prayer. What did he want God to do?

In addition to being a psalm of confession, this is also a psalm of lament, a type of prayer that draws us closer to God when we are suffering or in pain (which we will talk more about in a couple weeks). Lament is appropriate for prayers of confession because our sin should grieve us. (2 Corinthians 7:10) Sin separates us from God unless and until we repent. (Isaiah 59:1-2) It hurts us. It hurts others. What breaks God's heart should break our hearts too.

Have you ever thought about grieving your sin? What do you think that would look like?

Take a few moments to examine your heart and life. Are there places where you are intentionally, or even unintentionally, distant from God?

In "real time" in Psalm 38, we see David realize that God didn't separate Himself from David; David separated himself from God. But the good news is that God's kindness leads us to repentance. (Romans 2:4) He wants to remove anything that separates us from Him. That's why He sent Jesus. Jesus lived the sinless life we couldn't and died to make a way for our sins to be forgiven.

When you think about God's kindness leading us to repentance, does it make you want to be honest with Him about your mistakes and sins? Why or why not?

Psalm 38:9 gives us hope to cling to: "*O Lord, all my longing is before you; my sighing is not hidden from you.*"

When it feels like something is standing in between you and God, it can feel hard to discern where it's coming from. But a great first step is starting with confession. He already knows it all, and He will still forgive, redeem and restore you.

A PRAYER FOR YOU:

To close our study today, pray these words out loud to God from Psalm 38:21-22: "*Do not forsake me, O LORD! O my God, be not far from me! Make haste to help me, O Lord, my salvation!*"

David was known as a man after God's own heart. (1 Samuel 13:14) But David wrote today's psalm after the prophet Nathan confronted him for a very big problem he caused by committing a series of sins. David slept with a married woman and then killed her husband to cover it up (see 2 Samuel 11-12). Not exactly the poster child for following after God ...

Read 2 Samuel 12:13. What was David's response to Nathan?

Nathan's willingness to speak truth softened David's heart to repent before God. Instead of letting his offense or anger get in the way, he went straight to God to ask for forgiveness, cleansing and restoration.

How would you feel if you had a friend call out something you did wrong? Would you be angry or receptive? Do you have friends in your life who hold you accountable to God's Word?

David confessed. He stopped hiding. He did not blame anyone else. In Psalm 51, he asked God to *"blot out [his] transgressions"* (v. 1), *"cleanse"* him (v. 2) and *"deliver"* him from his guilt and sin (v. 14).

Let's reread Psalm 51:10-12. What three things did David ask God to do?

1. "_____ in me a clean heart, O God, and renew a right spirit within me." (v. 10)

2. "_____ me not away from your presence, and take not your Holy Spirit from me." (v. 11)

3. "_____ to me the joy of your salvation, and uphold me with a willing spirit." (v. 12)

NOTE FROM JOEL

David uses an incredibly important Hebrew word in Psalm 51 to describe the type of relationship we have with God. He said in Psalm 51:1 that he needed mercy from God *"according to [God's] steadfast love."* The Hebrew word translated as "steadfast love" is *ḥesed*, and it is rich with meaning.

The *ḥesed* of God refers to a type of love that is rooted in loyalty; it reflects the faithfulness of God. It is a love that is marked by covenant, which is where the idea of "steadfastness" comes from. It is constant and consistent. This is the love God has for us.

None of these things could David do on his own. He needed God to do a work within him. In his confession, he allowed God to renew and restore him.

And God answered this prayer for David. We know this because for the rest of his life, David sought the Lord, and the Lord continued to forgive him when he made mistakes again (e.g., 2 Samuel 24). What David did was sin, and it had consequences, but it **still** wasn't too much for God to forgive and redeem.

The same is true for you and me. Whatever mistake we feel too afraid to say out loud, the thing we fear someone finding out about us, it's not too much for God. When we confess, He is always faithful and just to forgive. (1 John 1:9)

If you are tired of hiding, come to Him. Tell a trusted friend, too, if you feel led. There is so much power in not having to hide. It reminds us that in Christ, we are free. And we can live like that is true.

A PRAYER FOR YOU:

Let's pray these words of Psalm 51:10-12 to end our study today:
"Create in me a clean heart, O God, and renew a right spirit within me. Cast me not away from your presence, and take not your Holy Spirit from me. Restore to me the joy of your salvation, and uphold me with a willing spirit."

To wrap up our week, let's look at one last psalm: Psalm 130. Read the psalm below, along with the notes and questions we've included alongside it, and consider how it relates to what we've studied this week. Let's deeply dig into the text to discover all God wants to teach us about prayer through these words.

Feel free to add your own notes, underlining and highlighting as you read! Consider underlining the things God does or will do, and highlighting the things David does or will do. Then make some notes: Who is more active? Who gives, and who receives?

PSALM 130
MY SOUL WAITS FOR THE LORD
A Song of Ascents.

¹ *Out of the depths I cry to you, O LORD!*
² *O Lord, hear my voice!*
Let your ears be attentive
to the voice of my pleas for mercy!

³ *If you, O LORD, should mark iniquities,*
O Lord, who could stand?
⁴ *But with you there is forgiveness,*
that you may be feared.

⁵ *I wait for the LORD, my soul waits,*
and in his word I hope;
⁶ *my soul waits for the Lord*
more than watchmen for the morning,
more than watchmen for the morning.

NOTES

Confession starts with admitting our need for God.

God will hear David.

David begs for mercy as he confesses; he is powerless.

The result of confession = forgiveness.

⁷ *O Israel, hope in the LORD!*
  For with the LORD there is <u>steadfast love,</u>
  and with him is <u>plentiful redemption.</u>
⁸ *And <u>he will redeem Israel</u>*
  <u>from all his iniquities.</u>

<u>God offers these things to those</u>
<u>who repent.</u>

REFLECTION QUESTIONS:

1. As you practice confession, what are the benefits you can remember that will help you keep going even when you don't want to?
2. Look especially at verse 5 of Psalm 130. How do these words encourage you, especially when you struggle to break a sin pattern in your life?

YOUR PRAYER:

Write a prayer below confessing your own imperfection and praising the greatness of God. Thank Him for Jesus and the beauty of forgiveness.

NOTES

NOTES

Week 2

WEEKEND REFLECTION

When Jesus taught His disciples to pray, He taught them to confess: *"and forgive us our debts, as we also have forgiven our debtors"* (Matthew 6:12).

Part of our daily rhythm of prayer is meant to include confession. Both the New Testament and the Old Testament make it clear that asking for forgiveness and acknowledging our sin is key, according to Jesus. Letting ourselves be searched and known by God deepens our intimacy with Him. (Psalm 139:23-24) We do not have to hide in shame. He has forgiven us and will forgive us because of what Jesus did on the cross!

Jesus also teaches us to forgive one another. But that word "forgiveness" is complicated. It's one thing to receive the forgiveness Jesus so freely offers, but it's also sometimes challenging to consider where we may need to extend forgiveness to someone else. Especially when someone has deeply wounded us with their words, betrayed us or broken our trust.

But just as our confession opens the door to forgiveness from God, we need to make space for it to open up forgiveness with others.

As you pray and think through this, consider the words of Colossians 3:12-14: *"Therefore, as God's chosen people, holy and dearly loved, clothe yourselves with compassion, kindness, humility, gentleness and patience. Bear with each other and forgive one another if any of you has a grievance against someone. Forgive as the Lord forgave you. And over all these virtues put on love, which binds them all together in perfect unity"* (NIV).

A PRAYER FOR YOU:

God, thank You that when I confess my sins, shortcomings and failures to You, You are faithful and just to forgive me, cleanse me and make me new. Just like David asked in Psalm 51, I ask You to make my heart pure. Help me to flee from temptation and choose righteousness. Remind me of the gift of Your grace, and show me how to extend that grace to others — because no matter what they've done or will do, no one is too far away for Your mercy and love to reach. In Jesus' name, amen.

51

3

thank you/

thank the

LORD/

you have/

the LORD has/

He has done/

In Psalm 86, "A Prayer of David," we get an intimate glimpse at a conversation between God and King David. David gives us a beautiful example of how to pray with thanksgiving, our prayer focus for this week.

How is thanksgiving different from adoration (which we learned about during Week 1 of this study)? Recall these definitions from Day 1: "Adoration is praise that originates from our hearts and that we pour out on God. Thanksgiving is our response to the love, blessing and compassion that flows from God onto us." In the midst of a scary and dangerous situation — his life on the line — David gave thanks in Psalm 86. Let's dive in so we can learn to pray with thanksgiving even when we're afraid, desperate and in need of a miracle.

In verses 1-7, David asked eight things of God. What are they?

1.

2.

3.

4.

5.

6.

7.

8.

It's surprising that David started a prayer of thanksgiving with eight requests of God. Because of this approach, what can we learn about the nature or format of prayers of thanksgiving? What does this reveal about God?

In verses 8-13, David shifted from petitioning God to praising Him for His power. At this point in the psalm, David hasn't explicitly thanked God for anything. In fact, in all 17 verses of Psalm 86, the word *"thanks"* is only used once (v. 12)! Yet we can start to see threads of thanksgiving woven through David's desperate appeal. How so? First, we need to understand something about thankfulness.

Thanksgiving is rooted in looking first at the past and then at the present. We can look at what God *has done* for us (and for others, like David) while also deciphering His hand in our lives *right now*.

> With that in mind, what makes this a prayer/psalm of thanksgiving? What signs of thanksgiving do you see?

NOTE FROM JOEL

The Ancient Israelites had a very specific vision of death. They believed death took place when the human soul separated from the body. The body decayed while the soul went to Sheol (שְׁאוֹל). In the Old Testament, Sheol referred to the place where both the righteous dead (like Jacob in Genesis 37:35 or Samuel in 1 Samuel 28:13-14) and the wicked dead (Psalm 31:17) would go. However, the righteous and wicked are located in two different places within Sheol.

These two locations are *"Hades,"* where the wicked suffer (Luke 16:23), and what the Bible refers to as *"Abraham's side"* (Luke 16:22), which seems to be a place of rest for the righteous as they await the Messiah, Jesus. It's interesting that there is even a *"great chasm"* or divide between the two places (Luke 16:26).

In the New Testament, the Greek word describing these places is "Hades." This is where things got interesting when the Hebrew Bible was first translated into Greek, called the Septuagint (LXX), by a group of rabbis/scholars. We can really think of the LXX as the first commentary on the Hebrew Bible. In the LXX, the Hebrew word "Sheol" is translated as "Hades": ᾅδης (same as the New Testament!). Why is this important? It shows us that when the New Testament talks about Hades, it has an Old Testament picture (Sheol) in mind.

Twice, David looked at what God had done in the past: *"all the nations **you have** made"* (v. 9) and *"**you have** delivered my soul from the depths of Sheol"* (v. 13, emphases added). These two past-tense acts of God serve as reminders that:

1. Because God made all the nations, He made the very men who had *"risen up against"* David (v. 14). Could He not then thwart their efforts to kill David? What's more, David says all nations *"shall come and worship before you, O Lord"* (v. 9). One day, every knee will bow before God. (Philippians 2:10-11)

2. God had saved David's soul from Sheol, the realm of the dead. His soul settled, David did not need to fear physical harm or death.

David also looked at who God is in the present: *"There **is** none like you among the gods, O Lord, nor **are** there any works like yours"* (v. 8, emphasis added).

Wrapping up his prayer, David offered a sneak peek of his complete trust in God for his deliverance. He trusted that God would not only do all he asked but also help and comfort him along the way. (v. 17) When we pray, let's remember our God is one of abundance. Not only will He save us, but He will help and comfort us, too … because His love for us is steadfast.

How can you model your prayers after this one? What words or phrases can you use in your own prayers?

A PRAYER FOR YOU:

Today, write your prayer of thanksgiving using Psalm 86 as a guide. Recall a time in the past when God came to your rescue, and review details of His deliverance in your prayer, letting God's past faithfulness guide you to thanksgiving.

At some point, we've all felt the sting of betrayal by someone we love. David did, too — and he let that sting drive him to cry out to God, who fights for us and will ultimately enact justice. Today we'll dig into David's prayer of thanksgiving to the God *"who delights in the welfare of his servant"* (Psalm 35:27).

In Psalm 35, David was under attack again — this time by men who sought to destroy him when he'd done nothing wrong. David's prayer reveals these were people he'd cared about at one time, (vv. 13-14) making their betrayal even more heartbreaking.

> Verses 1-3 are full of war language. Jot down the battle terms you notice. What was David asking God to be and do for him?

Just like Psalm 86, this dark psalm doesn't seem like a prayer of thanksgiving. It certainly reflects real life, which is often a mix of happiness and heartbreak. Still, we can always thank God because thanksgiving is an act of worship not dependent on our circumstances. Often, our prayers might sound like David's as we pour out our hearts while acknowledging what is true about God.

> Think of a time when you experienced heartbreaking circumstances. How did thanksgiving change your perspective of the situation? Or how could thanksgiving change your perspective now, looking back?

In this psalm, we see David giving thanks for God's heart for the poor, needy and weak. (vv. 9-10, 22-24) There are three instances of thanksgiving woven into David's pleas for deliverance, his lament over his enemies' hatred, and his petition for justice. These instances are tied to his body and soul, location, and time:

BODY AND SOUL: *"All my bones"* refers to wholehearted praise and joy. David's bones and his very soul rejoiced at the Lord's salvation. (vv. 9-10)

LOCATION: Once God saved David from his enemies, David promised to offer thanksgiving not only in private but in community, so others would come to know of God's deliverance and have the opportunity to trust Him. (v. 18)

TIME: David also promised to thank God continually. David would not soon forget God's deliverance. (v. 28)

List some ways you can thank God, your protector ...

WITH YOUR WHOLE BODY AND SOUL:

IN COMMUNITY:

CONTINUALLY:

Let's look at verse 27. What was David hoping would happen? Who would be glorified by this situation?

Even when others hate us, or just dislike us, *"without cause"* (vv. 7, 19), the Lord delights in our well-being, our happiness and our security. As you pray whispers of thanksgiving to God this week, you may also consider repeating the words of Psalm 91:2 (GNT): *"You are my defender and protector. You are my God; in you I trust."*

A PRAYER FOR YOU:

Dear Lord, I praise You for being my protector and fighting for me when I'm too weak. I confess I don't always ask You to fight for me — I try to do it myself. Forgive me, Lord. Thank You for delivering me when I'm poor and needy in spirit, for vindicating me when I experience the sting of injustice and betrayal. Please rescue me from destruction and contend "with those who contend with me" *(Psalm 35:1). In Jesus' name, amen.*

With only five verses, this psalm is not only the shortest thanksgiving prayer we'll study, but it's also very different from Psalms 86 and 35.

First, Psalm 100 is not attributed to David like the last two we've studied. Some Old Testament scholars attribute this psalm to Moses, but there are questions surrounding its authorship.[1]

Secondly, this psalm doesn't address the Lord directly, though it still holds elements of prayer. Verses 1, 2 and 4 are **invitations** to God's people while verses 3 and 5 describe both believers and the Lord.

Finally, Psalm 100 reflects a subtype of thanksgiving psalms called "enthronement psalms," which include Psalms 47, 93 and 95-99 (so we studied another enthronement psalm, Psalm 95, in Week 1).[2] Enthronement psalms are directly connected to corporate worship.

> In verse 1, who does Psalm 100 address? We can think of this as the "invitee." (Also see similar examples in Psalm 96:1, Psalm 97:1 and Psalm 98:4.)

Verses 1-2 of Psalm 100 offer three invitations or directions:
1. **Praise** God. (v. 1)
2. **Serve** God. (v. 2)
3. **Come** to God. (v. 2)

Then in verses 3-4, we're invited to:
1. **Know** God. (v. 3)
2. **Enter** God's gates. (v. 4)
3. **Give** thanks to God. (v. 4)

These threefold invitations come with important qualifiers. Not only are we invited to praise, serve, come, know, enter and give, but we're instructed to do those things in a certain way: with gladness, singing, thanksgiving and praise. (vv. 2, 4)

Think about how you serve God — whether in the local church or by serving your family, strangers, those in need, etc. Do you serve with gladness and praise? How could you serve God with deeper gladness and thanksgiving, coming to Him with a heart of praise?

Enthronement psalms differ from "royal psalms," which focused on events involving kings of Israel (weddings, installation of a new king, etc.), because Yahweh is the only King in enthronement psalms. This was a theological reminder that the king who sat on the throne in Jerusalem sat *under* the great King of heaven and earth. These Old Testament psalms also set the stage for our understanding of the enthronement of King Jesus. (Romans 8:34)

"Then comes the end, when he [Christ] delivers the kingdom to God the Father after destroying every rule and every authority and power. For he must reign until he has put all his enemies under his feet. The last enemy to be destroyed is death. For 'God has put all things in subjection under his feet.' But when it says, 'all things are put in subjection,' it is plain that he is excepted who put all things in subjection under him." (1 Corinthians 15:24-27)

What the Israelites sang as enthronement psalms are songs we sing today in acknowledgment that Jesus is King forever!

In verse 3, we see that a right perspective about our relationship with God helps get our hearts in the right posture for thanksgiving.

What does verse 3 say about who God is? What does it say about who we are to God?

Finally, in verse 5, the "why" of the invitation is revealed. Why should we accept this invitation to give thanks? The answer lies in three revelations about the Lord: He is good, He is steadfastly loving, and He is faithful.

In Psalm 86, we learned how great God's steadfast love is for us. In this psalm, we learn how long His steadfast love lasts. Note the length of time God's love endures according to Psalm 100:5! Also note who God's faithfulness extends to. (Galatians 3:28; Acts 10:34-45)

How does it make you feel to know God's love never ends and He doesn't discriminate when it comes to His faithfulness?

Finish writing the prayer of thanksgiving below, using the language of Psalm 100.

Dear God, You are my Creator and my Shepherd. With the rest of creation, I join in making a joyful noise to You today. Help me to serve You with gladness because of who You are and what You've done for me, knowing that it is an act of worship …

With 43 verses, Psalm 107 is the longest psalm we'll study this week. It may have been written during the Babylonian exile and features four testimonies of God's deliverance of His people.[1] Not only can we be encouraged by these testaments to God's power and dominion, but we can also learn how to model our prayers of thanksgiving after this one.

Read Psalm 107:4-32. What patterns do you notice among the four testimonies shared here? What did God deliver each group of people from?

Those who wandered:

Those who sat in darkness:

Those who were foolish:

Those who sailed:

Each testimony begins with some of God's people in crisis, in need of rescue. Then the people cried out to God in prayer, and He *"delivered them from their distress"* (vv. 6, 13, 19, 28).

The psalmist shares:

- **What God did in each situation.** For example: *"He led [the wanderers] by a straight way till they reached a city to dwell in"* (v. 7).
- **What we're to do in response to God.** For example: *"Let them thank the LORD for his steadfast love, for his wondrous works to the children of man!"* (v. 8).
- **Why our lives should overflow with gratitude for God.** For example: *"he satisfies the longing soul, and the hungry soul he fills with good things"* (v. 9).

Which testimony of God's deliverance resonates with you the most? What kind of deliverance do you need right now?

Another interesting detail to note is that in the second and third testimonies (vv. 10-16, 17-22), the people were experiencing crises caused by their own sin. Still, when they cried out to God in repentance, He delivered them just as He delivered the people in verses 6 and 28.

We are never too far gone for God to save us, and even when we walk through difficulties of our own making, He is faithful to rescue us. What a beautiful picture of God's mercy and grace!

If thankfulness is cultivated by looking at God's faithfulness in the past, as we learned on Day 11, and if this Psalm 107 prayer was indeed written during Israel's exile in Babylon, what event in Israel's history might verses 4-9 be about? And what about verses 23-32?

PSALM 107 SCRIPTURES	COMMONALITIES	EVENTS BEFORE BABYLONIAN EXILE
Verses 4-9		Numbers 32:13; Deuteronomy 1:6-8
Verses 23-32		Jonah 1:4-15; Jonah 2

The last 10 verses of the Psalm 107 prayer are about God's dominion over nature, people and governments. Not only does He care for the hungry, poor and needy, but He also executes justice on those who oppress them. This language is similar to David's in Psalm 86 and Psalm 35.

How can you model your prayers after Psalm 107? What words or phrases can you use in your own prayers?

Write your own prayer of thanksgiving today by *"consider[ing] the steadfast love of the Lord"* in your life (Psalm 107:43). Think about your testimony, how God saved you and brought you into His family and delivered you from crisis. Then form a prayer of thanksgiving modeled after the pattern of the four testimonies in Psalm 107, beginning with your crisis, how you cried out to God, and what He did to deliver you. End your prayer by thanking God for His steadfast love and for what you've experienced through His deliverance.

Today, let's read Psalm 138 together. We've included the text of the psalm right here in your study guide, and we've made some notes on verses 1-3 to get you started; take some time to annotate Psalm 138:4-8 yourself! There's no right or wrong way to do this, so let Scripture and the Holy Spirit guide you to notice, circle, underline, highlight and make note of anything God wants to teach you. Then thoughtfully consider the reflection questions below, ending with your own prayer of thanksgiving.

PSALM 138
GIVE THANKS TO THE LORD

NOTES

whole heart = not partial praise

¹ *I give you thanks, O LORD, with my* <u>*whole heart*</u>*;*
     before the gods I sing your praise;
² *I bow down toward your holy temple*
     and give thanks to your name for your steadfast love
and your faithfulness,
     for you have exalted above all things
     your name and your word.
³ <u>*On the day I called, you answered me;*</u>
     <u>*my strength of soul you increased.*</u>

David's actions:
-give   -bow down
-sing   -call

See Psalm 108:4, Psalm 115:1 and Psalm 117:2.

Verse 1: "'Gods' could refer to the pagan gods, in which case David was praising the true God in spite of their supposed presence."[1]

Answered prayer!

⁴ *All the kings of the earth shall give you thanks, O LORD,*
     for they have heard the words of your mouth,
⁵ *and they shall sing of the ways of the LORD,*
     for great is the glory of the LORD.
⁶ *For though the LORD is high, he regards the lowly,*
     but the haughty he knows from afar.

⁷ *Though I walk in the midst of trouble,*
     you preserve my life;
you stretch out your hand against the wrath of my enemies,
     and your right hand delivers me.
⁸ *The LORD will fulfill his purpose for me;*
     your steadfast love, O LORD, endures forever.
     Do not forsake the work of your hands.

A sometimes-overlooked aspect of this psalm is its cosmic nature. In Psalm 138:1 the psalmist says, *"before the gods I sing your praise ..."* Who are these "gods"? The Hebrew word *elohim* is plural, and it is used elsewhere in the Old Testament to reference supernatural beings, whether angels or demons (e.g., Exodus 12:12; Psalm 82:6). The Septuagint (LXX) translates the Hebrew *elohim* as "angels" (ἀγγέλων). The CSB translation of Psalm 138:1 says, *"I will sing your praise before the heavenly beings."*

The praise of God is not limited to an earthly context but is most natural in a cosmic (earthly and heavenly) situation because God is King of heaven and earth. In Psalm 138:2 we have a reference to the temple, which is often considered the throne room of God. In other passages of Scripture (for instance, Isaiah 6) angels are in constant praise of God. God's divine courtroom is made up of angels, and in their presence and God's, we sing the praises of God. In fact, when we take Isaiah 6 into consideration, we are actually joining the ongoing praise of angels as they cry out, *"Holy, holy, holy is the LORD Almighty"* (v. 3, NIV).

REFLECTION QUESTIONS:

1. David starts this prayer of thanksgiving by explaining how he praises God and then goes on to share what God has done. This order is not a natural cause-and-effect relationship of "God did this; therefore, I'll praise Him." Why do you think that is? What does this say about when and why we should give thanks to God?
2. Read Psalm 138:7 and Psalm 23:4, both written by David. How are these verses similar?
3. What language of thanksgiving stands out to you in Psalm 138? What verse do you find most significant, and why?

YOUR PRAYER:

Speak or write your own prayer of thanksgiving for how God has answered one of your prayers. If you have any doubt about His future faithfulness, take your doubt to Him today, knowing He can handle it.

NOTES

NOTES

Week 3

WEEKEND REFLECTION

This week, as we've studied prayers of thanksgiving in the book of Psalms, we've learned ...

- God loves us with a steadfast love. (Psalm 86)
- God protects us at all times, even when we're under attack by those who've betrayed us. (Psalm 35)
- God holds us in the palm of His hand because we belong to Him. (Psalm 100)
- God delivers and redeems us no matter what we're going through. (Psalm 107)
- God answers prayer and will always be faithful to us. (Psalm 138)

All of these are reasons to give thanks to God. But we've also learned that thanksgiving is not dependent on our circumstances; it's an act of worship (remember this from Day 12?). We may be in the middle of a terrible situation — maybe even one caused by our own sin (as we discussed on Day 14) — but we can still give wholehearted thanks to God because of what He's done in the past and what He's currently doing now, even when we can't see

it. As we learned on Day 11: **Thanksgiving is rooted in looking first at the past and then at the present. We can look at what God has done for us (and for others) while also deciphering His hand in our lives right now.**

How can we not feel thankful when we dwell on who God is to us, who we are to God, and the beautifully astounding fact that we can have a personal relationship with our loving, merciful Creator?!

After all, as we learned on Day 13, a right perspective about our relationship with God helps to get our hearts in the right posture for thanksgiving. That kind of thanksgiving is offered with *"all [our] bones,"* as David says in Psalm 35:10. Even if the bad situation we're walking through was caused by our own sin, we are never too far gone for God, and He is faithful.

Let's pray a prayer of thanksgiving, composed of verses from our thanksgiving psalms, to close out our week of study.

A PRAYER FOR YOU:

Dear Lord, You are good and forgiving, abounding in steadfast love to all who call upon You. You are great and do wondrous things, and You alone are God. "For great is your steadfast love toward me ..." (Psalm 86:13) I cry out to You in my trouble, confessing the ways I've rebelled against Your words. (Psalm 107) At the same time, my soul rejoices in You, exulting in Your salvation. "I will thank you in the great congregation; in the mighty throng I will praise you." (Psalm 35:18) May all the earth make a joyful noise to You; may we serve You with gladness and come into Your presence with singing! (Psalm 100:1-3) Though I walk in the midst of trouble, please preserve my life. "Do not forsake the work of your hands." (Psalm 138:8b) In Jesus' name, amen.

Word Study of *Yada*

(Hebrew for "Give Thanks")

The Hebrew verb for "give thanks" is *yada* (pronounced "yaw-daw"). Generally, it means "to throw, shoot, or cast," but in specific contexts, it can mean "to give thanks or praise." It can also mean "to confess sin."[1]

Interestingly, the verb *yada* is related to the noun *yad*, which means "hand." How is thanksgiving related to our hands? Think of how we raise or extend our hands in praise and worship — it's the same idea! When we praise God, throwing our hands up, we are thanking Him for who He is and what He's done as well as declaring in faith what we believe He'll do in the future.

Yada appears 114 times in the Old Testament, which was originally written in Hebrew (unlike the New Testament, which was written in Greek) — and the book of Psalms contains 64 instances of *yada*. That's more than half of all the biblical usages!

There are two notable instances of *yada* outside of psalms. One is when Leah, the wife of Jacob, birthed her fourth son, Judah, saying, *"This time I will praise* [yada] *the LORD."* (Genesis 29:35a).

The second notable instance is when David prayed *"on the day when the LORD delivered him from the hand of all his enemies, and from the hand of Saul"* (2 Samuel 22:1). David said: *"For this I will praise* [yada] *you, O LORD, among the nations, and sing praises to your name"* (v. 50).

See below the psalms in this study that include the word *yada* and the corresponding weeks you'll study those psalms.

WEEK 1   Psalm 145:10, *"All your works shall **give thanks** to you, O Lord, and all your saints shall bless you!"*

WEEK 2   Psalm 32:5, *"**I acknowledged** my sin **to you**, and I did not cover my iniquity; I said, '**I will confess** my transgressions to the Lord', and you forgave the iniquity of my sin. Selah"*

WEEK 3   Psalm 35:18, *"**I will thank you** in the great congregation; in the mighty throng I will praise you."*

Psalm 100:4b, *"**Give thanks** to him; bless his name!"*

Psalm 107:1, *"**Oh give thanks** to the Lord, for he is good, for his steadfast love endures forever!"*

Psalm 107:8, 15, 21, 31, *"**Let them thank** the Lord for his steadfast love, for his wondrous works to the children of man!"*

Psalm 138:1, *"**I give you thanks**, O Lord, with my whole heart; before the gods I sing your praise ... "*

Psalm 138:4, *"All the kings of the earth **shall give you thanks**, O Lord, for they have heard the words of your mouth ..."*

WEEK 4   Psalm 142:7a, *"Bring me out of prison, **that I may give thanks** to your name!"*

WEEK 6   Psalm 106:1b, *"**Oh give thanks** to the Lord, for he is good, for his steadfast love endures forever!"*

Psalm 106:47, *"Save us, O Lord our God, and gather us from among the nations, **that we may give thanks** to your holy name and glory in your praise."*

Psalm 28:7, *"The Lord is my strength and my shield; in him my heart trusts, and I am helped; my heart exults, and with my song **I give thanks to him.**"*

Psalm 33:2, *"**Give thanks** to the Lord with the lyre; make melody to him with the harp of ten strings!"*

cry /

despair/

pity /

broken /

anguish /

distress /

loathe /

mourn/

"How are you?" asks the cashier scanning your bread.

"OK," you say, all the while thinking, *Trust me — you don't want to know.*

"That's good." She nods, polite but distracted.

"How are you?"

"Good."

"Good," you echo, searching for the meaning of the word. You want to cry. Or kick or scream or do anything but watch this stranger calmly bag your spaghetti as if you're not barely surviving the hardest week of your life.

Have you been there? When our hearts are broken and we're desperate for hope, we long for a safe place to pour out our pain, but often the world seems full of strangers.

That's why we need Psalm 102. This prayer reminds us we can tell God the truth when we're not OK. In fact, *He wants to know* — so we don't have to choose between praying honestly and praying faithfully to Him. We can choose to lament, which will be our prayer focus this week.

What is lament? How would you define it, and how does it make you feel?

A lament is more than a sad prayer. Pastor Matt Boga says to lament is to "tell God about your pain ... the good things lost, and the new pains found, but do so with a confident and eternal hope."[1]

With this in mind, let's look at Psalm 102:3-11. Since God is all-knowing, no one can give Him new information. So why do you think the psalmist described his pain to God in excruciating detail?

If you've ever wept in the arms of a friend on your worst day, you know these moments are about intimacy, not information. Because of who He is, weeping in God's arms has an exponentially greater effect: Lament doesn't reveal anything new to God, but it invites God to reveal Himself anew to us in our pain.

> After reading Psalm 102, what would you say God revealed to the psalmist through his lament? Did this revelation change the *circumstances* of the psalmist's suffering or change his *perspective* on his suffering?

NOTE FROM JOEL

The all-knowing aspect of God is theologically referred to as His omniscience. This word comes from Latin: *omni* meaning "all" and *scientia* meaning "knowledge." More specifically, this deals with God's perfect knowledge of Himself and all things He has created. Because God is the creator of all things, He thus knows all things.

This means there are no limits to God's knowledge. God knows everything present, (Psalm 33:13-15) past (Job 38:4-5) and future. (Psalm 139:4; Isaiah 46:10; Matthew 26:34) As a note of comfort, the implication is that God can never be caught off guard. He is not surprised by the events of the world. God is fully aware, and in His omniscience He is working all things together for the good of those who love Him and toward His ultimate glory. (Romans 8:28)

If you've ever felt like God wasn't answering your prayers because He didn't change your circumstances ... how does Psalm 102 offer a new way to look at these prayers?

Some scholars theorize that the writer of Psalm 102 was an Israelite who lived during the 70-year Babylonian exile God foretold through the prophet Jeremiah. Jeremiah described a burned-out landscape of ashes, fire and waste places (see Jeremiah 25) much like Psalm 102 depicts.

Yet what hopeful promise did God make to His exiled people in Jeremiah 23:3-4?

How might this help us understand the hopeful shift in the psalmist's lament starting in Psalm 102:12 (*"But you, O LORD ..."*)?

In the end, what we know about Psalm 102 is that its writer suffered — but not without hope. Despair even stopped him from sleeping and eating, (vv. 4, 7) but it did not stop him from praying, which reminded him nothing can stop God.

A PRAYER FOR YOU:

God, when I look at my life today, I see withered grass and waste places. (Psalm 102:4-6) Sometimes my bones feel like they're burning inside me, but no one can see it. (v. 3) Honestly, I am not OK. I know I can't hide my pain from You — I want to tell You about it so You can reveal Yourself to me through it. You are "enthroned forever" and You "endure throughout all generations" (vv. 12, 24). Help me remember that all suffering has an end; only You are endless. In Jesus' name, amen.

Psalm 10 begins with questions:

1. "WHY, O LORD DO YOU _____ _____ _____?" (V. 1A)

2. "WHY DO YOU _____ _____ IN TIMES OF TROUBLE?" (V. 1B)

Sound familiar? Many of us have asked God some version of these questions when evil seems to be winning the battle for control of our lives and our world ... or maybe we've wanted to ask these questions but weren't sure we should. How could we accuse God of being unresponsive?

Well, let's look closer: Psalm 10 is not an accusatory prayer. It's a questioning one. Yes, the psalmist expresses confusion about why God seems distant from human suffering — but he also demonstrates faith. Where we look for answers to our questions shows who we trust, and this psalmist trusted God, even when he didn't understand Him.

> How do the psalmist's questions to God (vv. 1, 13) compare to the wicked man's *assumptions* about God in verses 4, 6 and 11? What is the difference?

At times, the psalmist and the wicked man's observations about God are actually similar (for example: *"Why do you hide yourself"* in verse 1 and *"He has hidden his face"* in verse 11), but their heart postures are completely opposite. Assumptions come from pride in our own knowledge. Questions require humility: We have to admit we don't know. This is arguably the most vulnerable posture we can take in prayer — and that makes it perfect for lament.

> What questions about justice and evil are troubling you today? Write them below. Have you ever prayed through these questions with the Lord?

When we've been devastated by evil schemes like Psalm 10 describes, it's painful to see the schemers go unpunished. We feel confused, even infuriated, which may tempt us to pray vengefully — like how Jesus' disciples once wanted to pray for *"fire to come down from heaven and consume"* their offenders (Luke 9:54).

> Read the whole story in Luke 9:51-56. How did Jesus respond?

NOTE FROM JOEL

Theologically, these are referred to as questions of theodicy. The English word "theodicy" comes from two Greek words — *theos*, meaning "God," and *dikē*, meaning "justice" — which could be literally translated as "divine justice."[1] There are many attempts to answer such questions, but the way God does so in the book of Job may be the most helpful. Rather than focusing on the logic of *why*, God assures us of *who*. In other words, God teaches us that it is often unhelpful to fixate on *why* there is so much bad in the world. We have limited knowledge, and our limits show up significantly when it comes to the problem of evil. A more fruitful exploration is *who* holds all of creation together. While the present may be hard, all is working together in redemptive history toward an ultimate good.

For Job, this "good" was the first advent of Christ in the incarnation — Jesus sent to us. For us, it is the second advent of Christ — Jesus returning to us.

Of course, this doesn't mean Jesus is uninterested in justice. What *"day"* does He mention in Matthew 12:36 and Matthew 10:15? What will happen on that day?

When we pray for God to *"call ... wickedness to account"* (Psalm 10:15), we do so trusting that He will right every wrong — whether **today** or on **Judgment Day**. Moreover, we remember that we ourselves are wicked sinners who have benefitted from God's mercy.

According to theologian Thomas Hartwell Horne, the wicked person in Psalm 10 "wants no prophet to teach him, no priest to atone for him, no king to conduct for him; he needs neither a Christ to redeem, nor a Spirit to sanctify him; he believes no Providence, adores no Creator, and fears no Judge."[2]

> Here's a hard question: Do you remember when this was true of you, before you knew Christ? How might this shape your prayers about injustice? (Also see 2 Peter 3:9.)

Ultimately, God answered this psalmist's prayer not by resolving his questions about evil but by revealing His authority over evil. Though God doesn't always tell us what **we** want to know about why wickedness seems to be winning on earth, He does tell us what **He** wants us to know: that He is *"king forever and ever"* (Psalm 10:16). We can trust Him with our questions because He is the perfect Judge who takes justice *"into [His] hands"* (v. 14) — and the Helper, Listener and Comforter who sustains us until then.

A PRAYER FOR YOU:

Lord, I don't understand why evil people seem to get away with murdering, abusing and crushing the helpless. (Psalm 10:8-10) It leaves me with a lot of questions. But my questions will only harden my heart if I don't bring them to You, so please give me courage to ask them humbly — not making demands about how You "should" answer but truly opening my heart to You and trusting Your goodness. Increase my faith to believe that evil ultimately does not win. You do. In Jesus' name, amen.

After the vivid descriptions of evil, sorrow and suffering we've read this week, the opening verses of Psalm 90, which praise God's eternal goodness and power, might not seem much like a lament. But by the time we get to verse 3, we see even these praises are mingled with pain, as God's eternity *"from everlasting to everlasting"* (v. 2) contrasts sharply with human mortality — from dust to dust. (v. 3)

Psalm 90 is a prayer of grief. In fact, theologian John Piper refers to it as a "death rehearsal."[1]

> What do you think this means? What phrases or ideas about death stand out to you in Psalm 90?

Psalm 90 is widely attributed to Moses, who led God's people from their exodus out of Egypt until their entrance to the promised land — including 40 years of wandering in the desert because they rebelled against God. This wandering may be reflected in the psalm's imagery: *"watch[ing] in the night,"* as Israelites would have done around the campfire (v. 4); grass that *"fades and withers,"* as they would have seen in the desert (vv. 5-6); and days spent *"under [God's] wrath"* (v. 9).[2]

> Read Numbers 14:33-35. How does this help you understand what Moses may have been mourning in Psalm 90?

Moses was well-acquainted with grief, and his pain was much like what we face today. In Psalm 90:10 alone, he lamented two all-too-familiar sorrows:

1. Life always feels too short. Even if *"the years of our life are seventy, or even by reason of strength eighty,"* they are *"soon gone."*

2. Life is full of hard work, challenges and problems (*"toil and trouble"*), which make our fleeting lives difficult.

Which of these sorrows is hardest for you to process today? Take a moment to tell God (or better yet, ask Him) why.

Death is certainly cause for lament. It's been *the* cause for lament since the garden of Eden. (Genesis 2:17) And none of us are born knowing how to process it: That's why Moses asked God to ***"teach us*** *to number our days that we may get a heart of wisdom"* (Psalm 90:12, emphasis added).

Praying for wisdom is an easy "yes" — but it's hard to pray for that wisdom to be learned through a holy appreciation of our few and difficult, yet eternally valuable, days on earth. Moses prayed the hard prayer.

And so did Jesus. (Mark 14:36) Christ set the ultimate example for us by grieving His own impending death on the cross yet following God faithfully every day of His life:

1. Jesus said, *"I am with you for only a short time"* (John 7:33, NIV). He lived less than half of what Moses said was a brief life. (Psalm 90:10) **But in 33 years, He changed the world by serving others in radical obedience to His Father.**

2. Jesus' life was marked by sorrow, hardship and pain from the day He was born. (Matthew 2:13; Matthew 12:14; John 11:33-35) But ***"for the joy that was set before him [He] endured the cross"*** **(Hebrews 12:2). And then in His resurrection, He defeated death forever!**

   In Psalm 90:15, what did Moses pray?

Because of Jesus, we know God has answered this prayer. In Christ, our eternal blessings will not only be *"as many"* (Psalm 90:15) as our present sufferings ... He promises *"an eternal weight of glory beyond all comparison"* (2 Corinthians 4:17).

A PRAYER FOR YOU:

Father God, thank You that You answer brokenhearted prayers. Please help me to remember this about You, especially when I feel devastated by how short and how difficult life seems. When my heart is crushed by grief for the ones I've lost and by fear of future losses, I dread numbering my days. But I trust You to teach me how to do this in a way that brings wisdom and eternal hope. (Psalm 90:12) Thank You for the opportunity to learn from You. In Jesus' name, amen.

IF I DON'T FEEL SAD RIGHT NOW, DO I STILL LAMENT?

Prayers of lament are not only a way to faithfully process life's hardest questions and emotions; they're also a kind of spiritual discipline. Lament is as much a part of following Jesus as confession or thanksgiving — though we don't often encourage one another to lament in the same way we encourage accountability or gratitude.

Of course, Scripture tells us to *"rejoice in the Lord"* (Philippians 4:4) because we have so much to celebrate in Christ! But here on earth, there is also much to grieve, and it's good to remember that for several reasons:

1. LAMENT PREPARES US FOR FUTURE SORROW.

"For everything there is a season, and a time for every matter under heaven: a time to be born, and a time to die ... a time to weep, and a time to laugh; a time to mourn, and a time to dance ..." (Ecclesiastes 3:1-4)

If we think of lament as a "last resort" prayer, to be prayed only during the hardest moments of life, we can start to think of hardship itself as exceptional, something we can hopefully avoid if we live well and pray the "right" prayers the rest of the time. Yet Jesus Himself tells us, *"In this world you will have trouble."* Lament teaches us to expect these troubles — but not to fear them, for Christ has *"overcome the world"* (John 16:33, NIV).

2. LAMENT PROMPTS US TOWARD COMPASSION.

"Rejoice with those who rejoice, weep with those who weep." (Romans 12:15)

We don't lament just for ourselves; we lament for others who are suffering even when we aren't. When we're in a great mood, the last thing we may want to do is pray for our newly widowed neighbor, our co-worker struggling with depression, or people affected by natural disasters in a nation thousands of miles away ... but the ministry of our prayers is eternal. After all, the command to *"weep with those who weep"* in Romans 12:15 follows the command to *"bless those who persecute you"* (v. 14) — not because either is easy but because both are holy.

3. LAMENT PIVOTS OUR PERSPECTIVE TOWARD ETERNITY.

"But woe to you who are rich, for you have received your consolation. Woe to you who are full now, for you shall be hungry. Woe to you who laugh now, for you shall mourn and weep." (Luke 6:24-25)

Sometimes we don't "feel like" lamenting because we're a bit too comfortable with life in this world — which is only temporary. Even our joy on earth is not meant to distract us from the reality that creation is *"groaning ... and not only the creation, but we ourselves"* while we await Jesus' return (Romans 8:22-23). As we lament that the world is horribly broken, we also anticipate the end of all lament, when Christ will redeem His creation forever just as He has promised! (Revelation 21:4)

Do you have a favorite worship song? Maybe it's an old spiritual your grandma used to hum while folding laundry, a hymn that gives you chills, or a new praise song on the radio that offers much-needed hope.

What probably doesn't come to mind is Psalm 22: *"I am poured out like water, and all my bones are out of joint; my heart is like wax; it is melted within my breast"* (v. 14).

Not quite "Amazing Grace," is it?

That's why it's fascinating that Psalm 22 includes instructions "to the choirmaster," suggesting psalms like this one may have been sung or recited by soloists in temple assemblies.[1] This approach seems to suit Psalm 22 — one man's lonely lament. But importantly, the psalm itself also draws attention to *"the great congregation"* of God's people (v. 25), describing the psalmist, David, as singing *"in the midst of the congregation"* (v. 22).

> How does this image of God's people surrounding the lonely psalmist change your perspective on his prayer of affliction in verses 1-18?

> How does this change your perspective on your affliction and your prayers?

In verse 16, David groaned, *"a company of evildoers encircles me."* But as David prayed, God reminded him that he was part of a greater company: a Kingdom of faithful fellow sufferers *"who seek [and] shall praise the LORD"* (v. 26). As Christian therapist and author K.J. Ramsey says, lament "guide[s] our whole selves to participate in ... the gospel story of interdependence."[2] And there's perhaps no better example of this than Psalm 22, as David's suffering drew him near not only to God's people but to God's own Son.

Complete the chart below to highlight a few of many ways Psalm 22 prophesied Jesus' suffering on the cross:

GOSPEL ACCOUNTS OF JESUS' CRUCIFIXION	PROPHECY IN PSALM 22
Matthew 27:39-43	
John 19:23-24	
Matthew 27:46	

The gospel changes everything! This includes our prayers of lament. Because he hoped in Jesus, the most alone David ever felt was actually the least alone he'd ever been. On earth, his clearest view of heaven was seen through tear-filled eyes. And the same is true for us: When we cry out, *"My God, my God, why have you forsaken me?"* (Psalm 22:1; Matthew 27:46), we speak the very words of Jesus Christ — who is our Savior and Immanuel, **God with us.** (Matthew 1:23)

According to Isaiah 53:4, whose grief did Jesus bear? Whose sorrows did He carry?

Friend, Jesus suffered for you, and He suffers with you. You are never alone. In Christ, we weep together and hope together on our hardest days, declaring that our worship does not come from our circumstances or even our feelings: *"From you [God] comes [our] praise in the great congregation"* (Psalm 22:25).

NOTE FROM JOEL

As we look to the cross, it is good for us to pause and consider the depth of loneliness Jesus felt as He not only endured the physical pain of the cross but absorbed the spiritual pain of sin in atonement for humanity. Jesus always enjoyed and experienced the presence of the Father and the empowerment of the Spirit. Yet on one day in His human existence, He experienced utter loneliness.

In Matthew 27:46, Jesus cried out not in triumph but in agony. Jesus was abandoned by His disciples, (Matthew 26:56) rejected and denied, (Matthew 26:69-75) and the religious rulers and Israelites all turned on Him (Matthew 26:57-68) as the Romans tormented Him. (Matthew 27:27-31)[1] Yet this darkest day of human history brought about the victory of Jesus so you and I would *never* have to be alone ever again.

A PRAYER FOR YOU:

Lord, sometimes it seems like I'm the only person who knows how it feels to hurt this much. I feel alone. But Your Word says when trouble is near, You are nearer. (Psalm 22:11, 24) Thank You that Jesus' forsakenness on the cross means You will never forsake me. Thank You for sovereignly using this psalm to comfort David thousands of years ago, prophesy Jesus' sacrifice, and give me hope today. If You can do that, I know You can "deliver my soul" (v. 20). In Jesus' name, amen.

To wrap up our week, let's look at one last psalm: Psalm 142, another lament of David. Read the psalm below, along with the notes and questions we've included alongside it, and consider how it relates to what we've studied this week. Add your own notes, underlining and highlighting as the Lord teaches you through this prayer.

PSALM 142

A MASKIL OF DAVID, WHEN HE WAS IN THE CAVE.

A Prayer.

¹ *With my voice I cry out to the LORD;*
 with my voice I plead for mercy to the LORD.
² *I pour out my complaint before him;*
 I tell my trouble before him.

³ *When my spirit faints within me,*
 you know my way!
In the path where I walk
 they have hidden a trap for me.
⁴ *Look to the right and see:*
 there is none who takes notice of me;
no refuge remains to me;
 no one cares for my soul.

⁵ *I cry to you, O LORD;*
 I say, "You are my refuge,
 my portion in the land of the living."
⁶ *Attend to my cry,*
 for I am brought very low!
Deliver me from my persecutors,
 for they are too strong for me!
⁷ *Bring me out of prison,*
 that I may give thanks to your name!
The righteous will surround me,
 for you will deal bountifully with me.

NOTES

See 1 Samuel 22:1 and 1 Samuel 24:1-3

Complaint before God is not the same as **complaint against** God.

David doesn't name those who are causing him pain in this psalm. This makes it easy for us to pray these words (whoever "they" may be for us) — and it also highlights the importance of the only name that does appear in Psalm 142: God's name.

Underline the uses of God's covenant name, *LORD*, in Psalm 142.

What a contrast: prison vs. refuge. A prison protects those outside from those inside, but a place of refuge does the opposite. What might this tell you about God?

The Hebrew word *ṭiḡ-mōl*, translated *"you will deal bountifully,"* is similar to the word *way-yiḡ-mōl* used in Numbers 17:8 to describe Aaron's wooden staff miraculously bearing almonds. Could this image of dead wood becoming fruitful by God's power relate to David's prayer for God to redeem his suffering?

REFLECTION PROMPTS:

- What truths from this week's study is God reinforcing as you read Psalm 142?
- What new truths about prayer in suffering is God revealing to you in Psalm 142? (Flip back to Day 16: Has your definition of "lament" changed? How?)

YOUR PRAYER:

Whether you need God to be your refuge in your current suffering, prepare your heart for future suffering, or soften your heart toward the suffering of others, write your own prayer below using Psalm 142 as inspiration.

NOTES

NOTES

Week 4

WEEKEND REFLECTION

Sometimes it feels overwhelming to talk to God about the most excruciating parts of our lives. The ones that pierce us so deeply it's hard to talk about them at all because just saying the person's name ... the diagnosis ... the date of the accident ... feels like another trauma. The ones that leave us so confused and angry we consider them unmentionable or even unthinkable. But hopefully it's been comforting to see that the psalmists withheld none of their complicated feelings in their prayers; when their bones were burning (Psalm 102:3) or their hearts were melting, (Psalm 22:14) they said so. But they also praised the kindness, nearness and sovereignty of a trustworthy God who will *"satisfy us in the morning with [His] steadfast love"* (Psalm 90:14) even on our worst days.

Every bit as undeniable as the pain in these prayers is the presence of God with those who prayed them. And that same God is with us today. He is with you right now. He hears your heart's cry. He mourns alongside you as sin and death ravage this world — the world where His Son suffered and died as a *"man of sorrows"* (Isaiah 53:3) — a world He has destined for eternal redemption because Jesus' grave, the ultimate pit of suffering, is now and forever empty! The psalms of lament in His Word are an example, a kindness and a gift to you, a guide for processing the crises of this life as "reasons for God's coming, not tokens of His distance."[1]

So even if you're not OK ...
Even if you have questions ...
Even if you're grieving ...
Even if you feel alone ...
Even if you're desperate for safety ...

Let's pray.

A PRAYER FOR YOU:

Lord, when we're suffering, it feels like our energy is consumed by problems we can't solve, pain we can't escape and people we can't save. But we want to be near You in every moment, even the most painful ones. Especially the most painful ones. So please show us Your grace toward messy, vulnerable, humbly question-filled prayers. By the power of Your Holy Spirit, help us to pray more often and more desperately so we can experience more of You. Please show us how to grieve together and grieve with hope. Remind us that we suffer not because You fail to protect us or because Your plans are thwarted by the enemy; "we suffer with [Christ] in order that we may also be glorified with him" *(Romans 8:17). The enemy is fighting a losing battle. You are victorious, and You are redeeming it all. In Jesus' name, amen.*

bread/
food/
sustain/
clothing/
satisfy/
thirst/
hunger/
provide /
supply/

5

This week we will be focusing on prayers of supplication. Supplication can be defined as the action of asking or begging for something earnestly or humbly. This category of prayer may be the one we're most familiar with, but it may also birth the most tension and angst for us as believers.

Why? Asking God for things we desire, big or small, requires deep trust in Him. We surrender to Him the potential outcomes of those prayers: the timing of His answer ... the delivery ... or if they'll be answered at all.

> Let's read Psalm 37:3 together: *"Trust in the LORD, and do good; dwell in the land and befriend faithfulness."* How do these words both encourage and challenge you in praying for things you want or need?

The next verse, Psalm 37:4, is probably one of the most common verses quoted in conversation about prayer. It's also one of the most misunderstood and misapplied verses.

> Write Psalm 37:4 below.

It's so easy to zone in on *"he will give you the desires of your heart"* and neglect the first part: *"Delight yourself in the LORD."* As we posture our hearts to talk to God in prayer, it's crucial for us to remember that prayer isn't a transactional process that exists only for us to get what we want. Prayer is an open door of communication so we can draw near to God, delight in Him and commune with Him, knowing confidently that He hears our every word.

Can we come to God with anything on our hearts, including our desires, wishes, hopes and dreams? Absolutely. But, friend, prayer is so much more than that. Think about it like this: If you had a friend you *only* talked to when you needed a favor, wouldn't your relationship begin to feel transactional?

Is there a time in your life where it was tempting for prayer to become overly transactional? How did this affect your relationship with God and your trust in Him?

In the opening line of verse 3, the Hebrew words hold significant meaning: *"Trust [bā·ṭāh] in the LORD [yhwh] ..."* The Hebrew word *bā·ṭāh* has to do with placing our confidence in someone. It implies reliance. And *yhwh* is the intimate Hebrew name of God; it was uniquely given to the Israelites as evidence of their special relationship with God. In fact, it was common when reading Scripture out loud that, as a sign of respect, the Israelites would not even say the name *yhwh* out loud. When I was learning Hebrew, my professor did something similar: When my classmates and I read Scripture out loud and we came across the name *yhwh*, he would have us substitute *adonai* (meaning "Lord").

This information is important because it lets us in on the special way God relates to His people. He wants to be known and proves Himself trustworthy. One way is through the revelation of His own special name to His people in the Old Testament. And today, we have something even greater in significance — the Word that became flesh: Jesus. (John 1:14) If we want to be reminded of the trustworthy character of God, we simply need to look at Jesus.

Theologian Charles Spurgeon says this: "Do not think first of the desires of thy heart, but think first of delighting thyself in thy God. If thou hast accepted him as thy Lord, he is thine; so delight in him, and then he will give thee the desires of thy heart."[1] It's not just about the prayers we're praying. The posture we're praying in is of equal importance ... a posture of humility, trust and patience.

> Look at verses 7, 18-19, 23-24 and 34 in Psalm 37. Write down any words that stand out to you regarding the posture of prayer you want to maintain in your heart.

As you continue on this 30-day prayer journey, remember the words you've discovered in Psalm 37 and the posture of prayer you want to walk in.

Finally, receive the prayer written for you below. Declare these words as you remember today that God hears every supplication you pour out to Him.

A PRAYER FOR YOU:

Heavenly Father, You know my every need. I know when I draw close to You in prayer, You hear me. Oh, Lord, it's so hard to trust You completely with things I want or worry about in current circumstances ... relationally, financially, emotionally, mentally, physically, spiritually. Remind me of the words of Psalm 37:7. I pray that I would be still before You and wait patiently for You through every single item on my prayer list. I trust You with the things most precious to me. I trust You with the unknowns in my future. I trust You with the things that stir up the most anxiety inside me. I trust You, Lord. Help me walk out this trust faithfully. In Jesus' name, amen.

The entire book of Psalms lends itself to prayer, but there aren't many psalms explicitly called "a prayer." Psalm 17 is one: It's titled "A Prayer of David." While we don't know exactly when David prayed these words, we can confidently say it was during a time of crisis.

In verse 1, David believed the cause he was bringing to the Lord was *"just"* and that his cries to the Lord were spoken from lips *"free of deceit."* This goes back to what we learned about confession and God's forgiveness during Week 2 of this study and what we said yesterday about the posture of our hearts when we enter prayer. Look at what David says in Psalm 17:3: *"You have tried my heart, you have visited me by night, you have tested me, and you will find nothing; I have purposed that my mouth will not transgress."*

> Go to Psalm 139:23-24, also a psalm of David. Notice David's posture toward the Lord and the humility he prays in. How might you invite the Lord to search your heart and thoughts like David as you bring Him your requests?

David invited God to test his heart; therefore, he knew he could enter a time of prayer with the confidence of a clean heart — not because he was perfect but because God's forgiveness is. Commentator James Boice says "open and unconfessed sin is a great prayer barrier. An upright life is a strong basis for appeals."[1] Boice also suggests the following questions for examining our hearts before we pray:

Am I being disobedient?
Am I being selfish?
Am I neglecting some important duty?
Is there a wrong I should first make right?
Are my priorities in order?

In keeping his heart swept clean, David was careful not to cross over into sin in the way he prayed about his crisis or his enemies.

What does Genesis 4:7 instruct us to do in regard to sin?

Even though David was in crisis, he didn't take matters into his own hands. *"From **your** presence let my vindication come! Let **your** eyes behold the right!"* (Psalm 17:2, emphasis added) David wanted the Lord to hear his cry, (v. 1) answer his words, (v. 6) protect him from what he was facing, (vv. 8-9) and deliver his soul from the wicked around him, (vv. 13-14) but he refused to take charge of these things *himself*.

This reveals David's deep trust in God. David very much believed that, at any moment, God could rescue him out of the troubling situations he was in — and he wanted to be delivered. But he trusted God to be the Deliverer.

Isn't this easier said than done? Especially when you're right in the middle of hard circumstances, feeling misunderstood, misrepresented or mistreated by others?

David understood this too.

Read Psalm 17:10-15. What was David saying about his enemies?

Look at Philippians 3:18-20 and jot down any similarities you notice.

In conclusion, David reminds us of four important things to remember about prayer, especially when we're walking through difficult circumstances:

1. We can bring our honest, unfiltered thoughts to God in prayer without crossing over into sin. (Psalm 17:1)
2. What we're experiencing may not feel like love, but it does not change God's unfailing love toward us. (Psalm 17:7)
3. God will continue to protect us even in times of crisis or trouble. (Psalm 17:8)
4. Hard and heartbreaking times don't have to prevent us from seeing and meeting with God. (Psalm 17:15)

A PRAYER FOR YOU:

Borrow these words from David and declare them as a prayer over yourself, your family, and any circumstances you're facing right now:

"I call upon you, for you will answer me, O God; incline your ear to me; hear my words. Wondrously show your steadfast love, O Savior of those who seek refuge from their adversaries at your right hand. Keep me as the apple of your eye; hide me in the shadow of your wings ..." (Psalm 17:6-8)

Psalm 143 is yet another prayer where David is crying out to God in a time of crisis. Again we see that the psalms are not cookie-cutter prayers written by perfect people in perfect circumstances. The psalms contain real words cried out by real people, sometimes in real hardship.

Does this realness bring you hope and comfort? Why or why not?

May we be reminded today to dig into real, honest prayers to God. We don't have to like what we're facing — even Jesus asked God to change the plan. (Mark 14:36) But like David, may we not allow what we're going through to dry up our thirst and desire for closeness with God. (Psalm 143:6)

"Hear my prayer, O Lord; give ear to my pleas for mercy! In your faithfulness answer me, in your righteousness!" David says in Psalm 143:1. Here, we see David desperately seeking God's attention while calling on His faithfulness and righteousness. In verse 2, he asked the Lord to deal with him not according to what he deserved (because of sin) but according to the Lord's mercy. Whatever David was walking through, he knew he would be lost without direction from God. He didn't try to manipulate God but simply prayed for God to act according to His character.

Is there a situation where you're asking God for direction right now? What have your prayers about this situation sounded like up until now?

Beginning in Psalm 143:5, David teaches us something so important about how to walk through hard times: He said, *"I remember ..."* In all he was processing, David paused to remember God's works and goodness from the past.

Why is remembering important? Because we so easily forget, especially when something currently doesn't feel good or God feels silent. When we're going through times of difficulty, those are the exact moments we should call our souls to *"forget not"* (Psalm 103:2), reminding our forgetful hearts that God has not forgotten us. The great theologian Charles Spurgeon describes it this way: "When we see nothing new which can cheer us, let us think upon old things. We once had merry days, days of deliverance, and joy and thanksgiving; why not again?"[1]

> Take a moment to journal about God's goodness and faithfulness you've experienced in the past. How does remembering the past inform your current doubt or uncertainties about the future?

David didn't just need the *"steadfast love"* of God (Psalm 143:8a); he also needed the guidance of God.

Let's look at Psalm 143:8b:

"MAKE ME KNOW THE _____ I SHOULD _____,

FOR TO YOU I LIFT UP MY SOUL."

In verse 10, David continues to pray: *"Teach me to do your will, for you are my God! Let your good Spirit lead me on level ground!"*

Let's dig deeper into three parts of supplication found in these verses:

SHOW ME (v. 8)
David didn't want to miss what God was doing or where God was leading. He said *"make me know the way,"* or *"show me the way"* (NIV). David asked for God to reveal Himself and for his own soul to remain attentive.

TEACH ME (v. 10)
David knew he needed God's instruction; he had the humility to ask God to teach him to do God's will.

LEAD ME (v. 10)

Moving forward, David prayed for God's *"good Spirit"* to lead him. He knew how prone he was, like all of us are, to go his own way. He didn't want to assume he knew where to go or what the right next step was. He needed God's leadership.

A PRAYER FOR YOU:

To close today, write your own prayer about a situation where you need God's direction. Incorporate these three phrases in your prayer:

Show me …

Teach me …

Lead me …

In Psalm 31, we find David not just in present suffering but in prolonged suffering: *"For my life is spent with sorrow, and my years with sighing ..."* (v. 10). Whatever he was praying for, the deliverance had not yet come to pass.

Can you relate? The painful aspect of prayers of supplication is the inevitable reality of waiting. Waiting for answers. Waiting for direction. Waiting for healing. Waiting for change.

In Psalm 31:9-13, what kind of waiting experience did David describe?

David's condition could be compared to what we find in the book of Job. His affliction was multilayered:

PHYSICAL
- *"my strength fails ... and my bones waste away."* (v. 10)

EMOTIONAL
- *"I am in distress; my eye is wasted from grief ..."* (v. 9)
- *"terror on every side!"* (v. 13)

SOCIAL
- *"I have become a reproach, especially to my neighbors ... those who see me in the street flee from me."* (v. 11)

MORTAL
- *"they plot to take my life."* (v. 13)

SPIRITUAL
- *"because of my iniquity ..."* (v. 10)

How do you relate to what David is saying? Have you experienced a time when waiting felt painful?

In his raw humanity, David relates to us. But by the power of the Holy Spirit, he leads us. After he cried out in his hurt, David said, *"But I trust in you, O Lord; I say, 'You are my God.' My times are in your hand ..."* (Psalm 31:14-15).

David was hard-pressed on all sides, but he was still pressing in spiritually, committed to God's will above all else. He said, *"Into your hand I commit my spirit"* (Psalm 31:5). These same words were later said by Jesus on the cross: *"Jesus, calling out with a loud voice, said, 'Father, into your hands I commit my spirit!' And having said this he breathed his last"* (Luke 23:46).

> Why is it challenging to commit our spirits to God and place our trust and our times into His hands?

David and Jesus' words show us both surrender and submission to God and His will. But surrender and submission grow increasingly difficult as we face difficult circumstances over a long period of time.

The longer we pray without seeing God's intervention ...
The longer we see our realities moving further from what we desire ...
The longer we cry out, doubting whether God hears us ...

This is why we must remember the humanity in the Bible. David understood the pain of life. Yet his closing words in Psalm 31:24 charge us: *"Be strong, and let your heart take courage, all you who wait for the Lord!"*

Friend, as you wait on the Lord to answer the cries of your heart, may you be strengthened by Him, and may you be filled with courage. For *"after you have suffered a little while, the God of all grace, who has called you to his eternal glory in Christ, will himself restore, confirm, strengthen, and establish you"* (1 Peter 5:10). As we suffer, we can be reminded of and encouraged by other champions of the faith, like David — and most of all, Jesus Himself — who understand the toll of the human experience.

What would it look like for you to *"let your heart take courage"* (Psalm 31:24) when you're waiting on God to answer you?

To wrap up our week, let's look at one last psalm: Psalm 121. Read the psalm below, along with the notes and questions we've included alongside it, and consider how it relates to what we've studied this week. Feel free to add your own notes, underlining and highlighting! Let's deeply dig into the text to discover all God wants to teach us about prayer through these words.

PSALM 121
MY HELP COMES FROM THE LORD
A Song of Ascents.

¹ *I lift up my eyes to the hills.*
   From where does my help come?
² *My help comes from the LORD,*
   who made heaven and earth.

³ *He will not let your foot be moved;*
   he who keeps you will not slumber.
⁴ *Behold, he who keeps Israel*
   will neither slumber nor sleep.

⁵ *The LORD is your keeper;*
   the LORD is your shade on your right hand.
⁶ *The sun shall not strike you by day,*
   nor the moon by night.

⁷ *The LORD will keep you from all evil;*
   he will keep your life.
⁸ *The LORD will keep*
   your going out and your coming in
   from this time forth and forevermore.

NOTES

Other things may bring temporary relief, but only YOU, Lord, are my Helper.

Look up! Eyes up! Off my circumstances and on my God!

The same God who MADE the heavens and earth is listening to my prayers!

God is always listening. He doesn't retreat or take breaks. He is constant.

See Psalm 91

Wherever I am, wherever I go, whatever my circumstances may be, the Lord watches over it all.

REFLECTION QUESTIONS:

1. In every supplication you bring the Lord today, how can you see Him as your Helper? (Psalm 121:1-2)
2. Look at Psalm 121:4. How do these words encourage you, especially in a time where God may feel quiet or even absent?

YOUR PRAYER:

Write a prayer below, placing in the hands of God everything you hope for and earnestly ask for.

NOTES

NOTES

Week 5

WEEKEND REFLECTION

As we conclude our week focusing on prayers of supplication, there is something we must acknowledge and create space to process: *grief.*

Chances are, as you are going through this study guide, you carry grief inside of you from these two scenarios:

1. You have been praying for an answer or solution in one area for a long time without seeing change.
2. In the past, you prayed about something important to you, and what happened in the end was the opposite of the result you were hoping for.

Friend, if this is true for you, the heartbreak you carry is real and is not ignored. God sees the grief you carry in your weary heart. It's OK to acknowledge that you have experienced or are currently experiencing disappointment in your prayer life. Remember: You can talk to God about anything.

As you continue to press in to these psalms and teachings, cling to the words of Lamentations 3:21-26:

"But this I call to mind, and therefore I have hope: The steadfast love of the LORD never ceases; his mercies never come to an end; they are new every morning; great is your faithfulness. 'The LORD is my portion,' says my soul, 'therefore I will hope in him.' The LORD is good to those who wait for him, to the soul who seeks him. It is good that one should wait quietly for the salvation of the LORD."

Even though there are parts of our stories where we carry grief, we can still have hope. God cares for us tenderly in our grief and through the tears we cry. Take a few moments to journal about some of the grief you may have experienced as you process past prayer requests that have gone seemingly unanswered. Before you journal, receive this prayer:

A PRAYER FOR YOU:

Father God, I know I am not hidden from You. You are close to me. As I think about prayer requests from my past that still linger with disappointment and grief because of their outcomes, I know You are close to me even here. I am making space today to grieve what needs to be grieved, process what needs to be processed, cry the tears I need to cry. But I will not let this grief create a wedge between You and me. I know You always have eventual, eternal good in mind, so I am choosing to trust You with all the details of situations I'm in. With every prayer request I bring to You. With everything that weighs heavily on my heart. Remind me that the lack of answers, change or intervention from You is not a punishment or a result of You ignoring me. I know You love me. I know You see me. I know You hear my every plea. I love You, Lord. Allow healing to take place as I continue to process these emotions. In Jesus' name, amen.

send/

friends/

your people/

bless /

help/

save/

care/

love/

Have you ever wanted to pray for someone but had one of these thoughts?

- *How? Am I even qualified?*
- *Does the Lord care if I'm praying for others?*
- *What difference would it make if I pray or they pray?*
- *The Lord isn't even answering my prayers for myself, so why would He answer when I pray for someone else?*

If so, we pray this week's study gives you some reassurance that you aren't alone. As we approach the conclusion of this study, we are going to dive into another type of prayer central to the gospel and the heart of Jesus Himself: intercession.

First, what exactly *is* intercession? Well, we actually see intercession every day. Intercession simply means going between or acting on behalf of another person. For example: A lawyer intercedes with the court on behalf of his or her client. It means stepping up for those who need it (even if they don't know they do!). Prayerful intercession means approaching the Lord on someone's behalf.

Let's begin our week by looking at an intercessory prayer for a group of people: the nation of Israel. In Psalm 106, our psalmist asked the Lord to help and save Israel in their time of need. He begged for the Lord to remember them, or in other words, remember His promise to rescue them from their enemies.

> Think of a group of people in your life who have not yet experienced deliverance from sin, or a group of people you care for who are widely suffering or rebelling. Is it your nation, community, co-workers, friends? Write it down below and keep this in mind as we move through today's questions.

Before he spoke his plea, the writer of Psalm 106 delved into Israel's history in verses 6-46.

> Write down some of the sins you see the psalmist confessing on behalf of his nation. When you reflect on the history of the people you want to pray for today, what sin or greatest need comes to mind? (You may consider your own sin as well.)

Write down some of the actions God performed for Israel, as recorded in Psalm 106. How have you seen God at work in the history of the people you want to pray for today?

Our history greatly informs our present. Reflecting on what we have experienced individually or communally can be difficult, but the ways the Lord has delivered us bring us toward praise!

Psalm 106:40-48 indicates this psalm was composed at the end of Israel's Babylonian exile (remember this from Days 14 and 16?) — but not yet at their deliverance. The Israelites were experiencing great hardship, but the psalmist did not overlook that God had already begun to have mercy on them. Though they were still experiencing persecution, the psalmist reflected on the goodness of the Lord and asked boldly in faith for Him to save Israel from captivity.

Read Ephesians 2:4-5. Why does God act mercifully toward us, just as He acted mercifully toward Israel? (Psalm 106:45)

Finally, the psalmist made his request. He cried out to God, much as you and I do when we have reached the end of ourselves. Let's face it: The psalmist couldn't control the actions of a nation, just as we can't control the choices of any group.

We cannot control any habitual sin patterns or widespread rebellion against the Lord. We cannot change the hearts of people to repent from their sin. We can't even persuade them to see their sin as sin.

But the psalmist asked the Lord for forgiveness and deliverance *anyway*. And we can plead for the Lord to change people's hearts (including ours) and grant mercy.

It takes faith to believe that the Lord is merciful and true to His Word and that Jesus loves our broken, sinful communities. We can step in boldly with this faith to pray for our friends, families or whole nations to repent and be delivered from sin, just as we have been delivered by Christ.

The Psalm 106 psalmist spent most of this prayer reflecting on the past. But in verses 47-48 he projected into the future.

What did the psalmist ask of the Lord, and what did he say he would *"give"*? How does this example inspire your own prayer?

Spoiler alert: The Lord DID deliver the Israelites and return them to their land. (Ezra 1:1-4; Ezra 5:13-15) What a merciful God!

A PRAYER FOR YOU:

Lord, You know the heart of each person in my life. And though we have been rebellious and sinful against You, I ask You to save us from our sin and bring us into Your redemption. Convict our hearts, and draw us to repentance. You are always present, knowing the depths of our suffering, and have walked in our history with us. Forgive us and deliver us from our sin. In Jesus' name, amen.

Jesus Christ:
The Great Intercessor

Sometimes we feel like we don't always have the best words to offer the Lord. When we feel this way, it might cross our minds … *Why should I pray for others?* It's a great question, with a simple answer: As believers, we intercede for others because Christ intercedes for us and has given us the Holy Spirit to help us pray. We are not powerless in Christ. Also, the Lord truly *wants* us to pray on behalf of others. Let's look at how this is true.

Christ is the example we are to follow. Look at three verses that show Jesus as the great Intercessor:

> *"My little children, I am writing these things to you so that you may not sin. But if anyone does sin, we have **an advocate with the Father, Jesus Christ** the righteous."* (1 John 2:1, emphasis added)

> *"Consequently, he is able to save to the uttermost those who draw near to God through him, since he **always lives to make intercession** for them."* (Hebrews 7:25, emphasis added)

> *"Who is to condemn? Christ Jesus is the one who died—more than that, who was raised—who is at the right hand of God, who indeed is **interceding for us**."* (Romans 8:34, emphasis added)

Charles Spurgeon says, "He seems to have thought of all [His people's] wants, of all their needs, of all their weaknesses, and in one long stream of intercession, he pours out his heart before his Father's throne."[1] What an advocate! Not only is Jesus petitioning on our behalf, but He also *took on* the punishment we sinfully deserved.

Without the intervention and advocacy of Christ, we would not have the gospel. Intercession is God's idea and Jesus' mission. And are we not called to be like Christ? (Read 1 Corinthians 11:1; Ephesians 5:1-2; 1 Peter 2:21 and 1 John 2:6 if you're not so sure!) It is a privilege to be able to shadow the role that Jesus Himself fulfills. It is a great blessing to be able to advocate for others just like Jesus does for us. By prayerfully interceding, we are becoming more like Christ.

THE HOLY SPIRIT

When God the Father sent the Holy Spirit after Jesus' ascension, (John 14:26; Acts 2) He gave us power for prayer. In intercessory prayer, we can have confidence that the Spirit is working and moving in us, and the Spirit is also praying for us.

> *"Likewise the Spirit helps us in our weakness. For we do not know what to pray for as we ought, but **the Spirit himself intercedes for us** with groanings too deep for words. And he who searches hearts knows what is the mind of the Spirit, because **the Spirit intercedes for the saints** according to the will of God."* (Romans 8:26-27, emphases added)

Before you pray, remember you have the Spirit. Ask Him to form and empower your prayers.

Think on this quote from Spurgeon as you spend time praying for others this week: "I pray you use it [intercessory prayer] on the behalf of the poor, the sick, the afflicted, the tempted, the tried, the desponding, the despairing; when thou hast the King's ear, speak to him for us."[2]

How often do you feel like you've tried and tried to help a loved one with something they're struggling with, but nothing you do is working?

Loved ones living with depression, family members struggling with addiction, rebellious children, or people who you just don't understand why they're doing what they are ... No matter how much you talk to them, how many resources you provide, it seems like nothing is helping.

That feeling is hollowing.

However, here's some really good news: You can't do it. But Jesus can. You are free from the pressure of saving someone from their hardship. **Savior is a role only Jesus can fulfill; He provides true healing and restoration.**

We find an example of this holy surrender in Psalm 60, which is set in a time of hardship for the psalmist, King David. He used this prayer to reflect on how broken he and his people felt but also to reflect on the victory God had given him in many battles.

> Read Psalm 60:1-10. Write down some emotions David may have been feeling. (This will take some interpretation: For example, in verse 9, you could say David felt lost or directionless.)

David was a beloved king chosen by God for God's purposes. Yet even David, who was anointed by the Spirit of the Lord, (1 Samuel 16:13) sometimes felt like he was alone and failing at helping his people. What is significant is what came next.

> Read Psalm 60:11 and fill in the blanks:

"OH, GRANT US HELP AGAINST THE FOE,

FOR _____ IS THE _____ OF _____!"

Let's get *really* honest with ourselves. In what areas of life have you been relying on human power to save you instead of God's power?

David called human salvation *"vain."* This means futile, useless, without value. If our pride gets involved, this truth about our efforts can actually hurt a bit. But in light of the gospel, it is so sweet. Second Corinthians 12:9 says Christ's power is *perfected* in our weakness. It is actually good that we cannot save others! We can bring God glory as *He* delivers those around us.

Psalm 60:12 says, *"With God we shall do valiantly; it is he who will tread down our foes."* To be valiant means to act bravely or courageously.

Friend, it's time to trade in vanity for valiance. We have such a deep desire to help our loved ones that it can be hard to relinquish control to God ... but God wants to tread down their foes and ours. Let's surrender to Him.

Use the lines on the left to list people and situations you have been holding on to too tightly. What or who have you been trying to save on your own? On the right side, write "belongs to God" as a symbol of handing over each person and situation to Him. (We've completed one set of lines for you as an example below.)

The health of my children   Belongs to God

Let's wrap up the day with the words of theologian Matthew Henry: "Oh, that we would learn to just trust in God; call upon Him for our help. Rather than looking to man, look to God ... It is a great day when I just yield to God all the issues of my life. And I trust Him completely."[1]

A PRAYER FOR YOU:

God, I trust that You will deliver my loved ones through their hardship, even if that looks different from how I desire. Thank You, Jesus, for releasing me from the pressure of trying to save them. [Spend some time praying through the list you made above, where you traded in your vanity for valiance in God.] *Today, I trust that You will tread down their foes and that You will comfort, convict and save my loved ones in need. God, You are good. In Jesus' name, amen.*

When we're praying for someone who is suffering, our prayers can feel desperate and conflicted. We may be full of hope but also experience despair and frustration while we wait for the Lord to intervene. Sometimes, we even find ourselves on our knees *begging* for the Lord to do something.

In Psalm 20, the nation of Israel felt compelled to pray for King David as he prepared to ride into battle. This psalm is what they prayed.

Imagine King David at the tabernacle of God, offering sacrifices to prepare for battle when he heard the people call out, *"May the LORD answer you in the day of trouble!"* (v. 1). Theologian Derek Kidner says this is "one of the most stirring of the Psalms, by its tense awareness of life-and-death issues soon to be resolved."[1]

You may feel this same awareness when your friends are struggling and desperately need you to pray for them.

> Read Psalm 20 in full, and then focus on verse 1. What is the *"day of trouble"* for your loved ones today?

> Read verses 1-5. What is the first word of every single one of these verses? How many times is this word used throughout the psalm?

The Hebrew root word used here in the phrase *"**May** the LORD **answer**"* (v. 1) is עָנָה (*anah*). It means to testify, to hear, to sing, to shout, to give account, to beg God to heed and answer.[2] The verb form here is called "imperfective," which means it also could be translated "may He pay attention" or "may He respond." When Israel prayed, *"**May the LORD answer** ..."* they were fervently asking the Lord to hear them and answer their prayers because they greatly cared for the one they prayed for.

Isn't this familiar? Psalm 20 gives us an example of how to come before God and pray for a loved one who needs Him — with conviction that He is listening. It's as if the people were believing in a promise God had given, though it hadn't been fulfilled yet.

When you come to the Lord in prayer for those who you know are facing a battle, consider praying this very psalm for them.

Using verses 1-3, complete the corresponding "may" statements. We can use this as a guideline for our prayers.

1. "MAY THE LORD _____ _____ IN THE DAY OF _____!" (V. 1A)

2. "MAY HE SEND YOU _____ FROM THE _____ ..." (V. 2A)

3. "MAY HE REMEMBER _____ _____ _____ ..." (V. 3)

Below are some blank "may" statements. Use these lines to write down how your loved ones need deliverance. When you approach the throne of God to petition for them, what are you specifically praying for?

1. MAY THE LORD _____

2. MAY HE SEND _____

3. MAY HE REMEMBER _____

Finally, here are three more blank "may" statements. Use these to think of how YOU need deliverance. How would you like a friend to be praying for you in your day of trouble? Consider asking a trusted friend or family member to pray for you based on these lines.

1. MAY THE LORD _____

2. MAY HE SEND _____

3. MAY HE REMEMBER _____

In the midst of great petition and making requests of the Lord, the psalmist(s) also took a moment to recognize the character of God as strong, merciful and greatly desiring good for His people. (vv. 6-8) This is our God!

Intercessors
Throughout the Bible

Intercession isn't just in the book of Psalms! Complete the following chart to observe different biblical figures prayerfully interceding and how God responded to this.

	WHO INTERCEDED?	WHO DID THEY PRAY FOR?	HOW DID GOD RESPOND?
Genesis 17:17-22			
Numbers 14:11-22			
Job 42:7-12			
Luke 23:32-34			
John 11:38-44			

Sometimes, doubt shows up like an unwanted companion. We doubt that our friends will stick with us in hardship. We doubt that someone close to us is going to keep their word. We doubt that our efforts as parents are going to be fruitful. The worst part is ... sometimes these doubts become a heartbreaking reality.

And then it's just a little easier to doubt that God is listening when we pray. Or doubt that God is who He says He is. Or doubt that the Lord will carry us through hardship. When we let doubt into our hearts, it is easy to think: *OK, I'll pray, but I doubt God is going to help me or those I'm praying for.*

When doubt creeps in, it is easy to forget who God is and why we can trust Him. But in the midst of prayer, especially prayer for others, evaluating the character of God and all He has done for us can remind us of the security we have in bringing our prayers to Him.

Psalm 28 reveals many characteristics of God through the recounting of His actions.

In the chart below, list the verses of this psalm that describe the characteristics of God.

THE LORD IS ...	VERSES OF PSALM 28 THAT SHOW THIS: (You can use the same verse more than once.)
Strong	
Just	
Merciful	
Attentive/Listening	

In Psalm 28, we see the Lord's character in action. In verses 7-8, David declared that he relied on the Lord's strength.

We, too, can confidently declare this:

"THE LORD IS MY _____ AND MY _____; IN HIM MY

HEART _____, AND I AM _____; MY HEART EXULTS,

AND WITH MY SONG I GIVE _____ TO HIM" (V. 7).

What a truth to hold on to! Charles Spurgeon encourages us in his application of this verse: "My dear friend, if you can say, 'The Lord is my strength,' you can bear anything and everything. You could bear a martyr's death if the Lord should be your strength. He could make a stalk of wheat to bear up the whole world if he strengthened it."[1]

In what areas of your life do you need the Lord's strength? In what areas do the people around you need His strength?

When we trust God as our strength, we can have confidence He will help us. This may look different than what we ask or expect, but remember: The Lord is faithful to those He loves. *"The LORD is the strength of his people; he is the saving refuge of his anointed."* (v. 8) Even if we are doubting, these truths affirm we have a good God who loves and helps us in our need.

When we are praying for a loved one, community, enemy or anyone else, we need the Lord to sustain us and them. So David reminded himself of God's strength to orient his heart before making his request.

Finally, David stated his petition for the Lord to be his people's strength. This is a prayer for those who need the Lord's guidance and provision.

Read Psalm 28:9. Who do you need to pray for who needs God to be their shepherd and carry them forever? Write down a few names.

We could add our own names to this list. If you are doubting the Lord's strength and provision for yourself and need prayerful intercession, send this psalm to a friend or family member and ask them to pray verse 9 over you as well.

Use the space below to write a prayer beginning with identifying who God is, then moving into prayer for those you listed above, asking God in His strength to shepherd and carry them forever.

You're at the end of this week and at the end of this study guide! Praise God for all the ways He has used your prayers over these six weeks! We will close our week of intercessory prayer by annotating Psalm 33. At the end of the psalm, you'll find a couple reflection questions to guide your annotations if you'd like, or feel free to use the blank space to identify whatever it is you see in this psalm.

We've identified some important actions, characteristics of God, repeated words and **interesting images** in the text. What does this psalm make you think and feel?

PSALM 33
THE STEADFAST LOVE OF THE LORD

NOTES

¹ *Shout for joy in the LORD, O you righteous!*
   Praise befits the upright.
² *Give thanks to the LORD with the lyre;*
   make melody to him with the harp of ten strings!
³ *Sing to him a new song;*
   play skillfully on the strings, with loud shouts.

⁴ *For the word of the LORD is upright,*
   and all his work is done in faithfulness.
⁵ *He loves righteousness and justice;*
   the earth is full of the steadfast love of the LORD.

⁶ *By the word of the LORD the heavens were made,*
   and by the breath of his mouth all their host.
⁷ *He gathers the waters of the sea as a heap;*
   he puts the deeps in storehouses.

⁸ *Let* all the earth fear the L*ord*;
  let all the inhabitants of the world stand in awe of him!
⁹ *For he spoke, and it came to be;*
  he commanded, *and it stood firm.*

¹⁰ *The L*ord *brings the counsel of the nations to nothing;*
   he frustrates the plans of the peoples.
¹¹ *The counsel of the L*ord *stands forever,*
   the plans of his heart to all generations.
¹² *Blessed is the nation whose God is the L*ord,
   the people whom he has chosen as his heritage!

¹³ *The L*ord *looks down from heaven;*
   he sees all *the children of man;*
¹⁴ **from where he sits enthroned he looks out**
   on all the inhabitants of the earth,
¹⁵ **he who fashions the hearts of them all**
   and observes all their deeds.
¹⁶ *The king is not saved by his great army;*
   a warrior is not delivered by his great strength.
¹⁷ *The war horse is a false hope for salvation,*
   and by its great might it cannot rescue.

¹⁸ *Behold, the eye of the L*ord *is on those who fear him,*
   on those who hope in his steadfast love,
¹⁹ *that* he may deliver *their soul from death*
   and keep them alive in famine.

²⁰ *Our soul* waits *for the L*ord;
   he is our help and our shield.
²¹ *For our heart is glad in him,*
   because we trust in his holy name.
²² *Let your* steadfast love, *O L*ord, *be upon us,*
   even as we hope *in you.*

REFLECTION QUESTIONS:

1. What does this psalm instruct us to do as a result of God's goodness?
2. What characteristics or roles of God are described in this psalm?
3. Where is the intercessory prayer in this psalm?

YOUR PRAYER:

Use the space below to write your prayer to the Lord, using Psalm 33 as inspiration.

NOTES

NOTES

Week 6
WEEKEND REFLECTION

Thank you for participating in this final week of our study of prayer through the book of Psalms. Wrapping up, let's turn our eyes toward Jesus and talk about what is true when we struggle to pray for others because we struggle to pray at all.

Friends, life can be *hard* — there is no getting around that. Sometimes in the midst of our own grief, lament, recovery, addiction or sinful patterns, we want to cry out in discouragement. We feel like we can't bring ourselves to pray for others because it is so hard even to pray for ourselves. We have nothing to give.

Remember this week when we looked at how Jesus and the Holy Spirit are great intercessors? (See page 112-113.) This truth is a great comfort when we feel this way.

There will be days when you need someone to intercede for **you**, but you lack the words to ask for help. On those days, remember these two things:

First, Jesus knows how you feel. He knows rejection, disappointment, ridicule, exhaustion, heartbreak, frustration, poverty, temptation and so much more. He knows your suffering. You are in the care of an empathetic God. The book of Hebrews reminds us of this:

"For we do not have a high priest who is unable to sympathize with our weaknesses, but one who in every respect has been tempted as we are, yet without sin" (Hebrews 4:15).

While the Lord loves for us to speak to Him and tell Him what is going on, even when our words fail, we can have confidence that He knows and cares.

Secondly, we can be confident that Christ is constantly interceding for us. He is bringing us back to Him. Remember the gospel, friends: Christ loves us so much that He became a man and sacrificed His very life so we could be united with Him. With a love that runs this deep, we can have confidence that He is speaking for us when we feel speechless. (Romans 8:34)

A PRAYER FOR YOU:

Lord, thank You for the ways You've challenged, equipped and encouraged me in prayer throughout the past six weeks. Help me not to forget what I've learned, and prepare my heart for when I am emptied out and without words to pray. When I sit before You silent, broken and hollow, fill me with Your comfort and peace. Jesus, You know my heart. You know my suffering. You have loved me despite my sin and washed me from it. So I pray for Your intercession today. You are the God of restoration. May You restore me and those around me. Bring us through our brokenness to Your glory. In Jesus' name, amen.

❀ *Praying* the Lord's *Prayer*

In addition to studying the book of Psalms, we can also look to Matthew 6 for instruction from Jesus on how to pray. If you've been around Christian circles for a while, you may have heard this passage of Scripture called "the Lord's Prayer."

Jesus meant for this prayer to be used as a daily guide for how to converse with God — not in a way that's legalistic or just checks a box but as a guide for our benefit. It's what the human heart needs every day: communion with God.

> *"Pray then like this:*
> *'Our Father in heaven,*
> *hallowed be your name.*
> *Your kingdom come,*
> *your will be done,*
> *on earth as it is in heaven.*
> *Give us this day our daily bread,*
> *and forgive us our debts,*
> *as we also have forgiven our debtors.*
> *And lead us not into temptation,*
> *but deliver us from evil.'"*

MATTHEW 6:9-13

Jesus' prayer lifts up God's will above His own. (v. 10) He establishes that the Lord will provide what we need daily. (v. 11) After that, He walks us through praying for forgiving hearts and the ability to stand against the temptations of the enemy. (vv. 12-13)

This is how we pray: In worship and thankfulness and praise, we ask for God's will, for what we need, for forgiveness, and for deliverance from evil.

We will readily admit we struggle to do this daily ... and maybe that's the very reason why we can slip into spiritual funks so easily. So we created this guided prayer space for you to really experience the power of the Lord's Prayer. Use this as your safe space for learning, processing, journaling and communicating with your heavenly Father. Together, we can lean into what Jesus taught us through this perfect example of uncomplicated prayer — simple words spoken from a humble heart to a good God.

Pray then like *this* ...

1. "... OUR FATHER IN HEAVEN, HALLOWED BE YOUR NAME."
(Matthew 6:9)

In the Old Testament, references to God as "Father" were limited and primarily used as an analogy rather than a personal name for God. So when Jesus addressed God as *"our Father"* in this prayer, His Israelite disciples would have been shocked by the relational intimacy. Calling God "our Father" is personal and opens the door for new understanding about our relationship with God. He isn't just our supreme authority; God is our heavenly Father.

God loves for us to draw near to Him and call out to Him as our Father. No matter what your relationship with your earthly father looks like, your heavenly Father wants a loving relationship with you. Friend, even though our hearts may get broken from the effects of sin on this side of eternity, God's goodness does not change. We must hold fast to the truth of who God is and His unchanging nature: He is a good Father.

PRAY:
Use the space below to pray, worship and declare how personal and close God is to you as your Father. This will help you remember who is on the other side of your praying: the God who intricately made you, loved you from the start, and has good plans for your life. "Our Father" relieves the pressure we put on ourselves to "impress" (or at least avoid "failing") God in our prayers. You can pray to Him as a beloved daughter — not trying to win His affection but knowing He gives it to you freely.

2. "YOUR KINGDOM COME, YOUR WILL BE DONE, ON EARTH AS IT IS IN HEAVEN." (Matthew 6:10)

The three sections here — *"your kingdom come," "your will be done"* and *"on earth as it is in heaven"* — are all wrapped up in a future promise. This means that as we pray, we look forward to the promise that awaits us: Jesus' return!

It's like sneaking into the kitchen while your mom makes dinner to "taste test" the meal. This advance taste sets our expectations and affirms our longing for the full meal promised to us. If we truly believe God's will is good and better than what we think we want right now, we won't reach for lesser things to temporarily satisfy us. If we know the meal will be so delicious and satisfying, we won't be nearly as tempted to fill up on candy bars in the minutes before the food is served.

However, this future promise comes with present responsibility for us to participate in God's Kingdom today. Why is this important? Because as we pray through this section, we are trading what we may want right now for God's will, which is always best in the long run. This prayer is our reminder that God's will is better than our short-term desires.

This is what it means for earth to be *"as it is in heaven."* We want to taste for ourselves His Kingdom that is to come. And we want to give others a taste as well through our lives of faithfulness, love and obedience to God.

PRAY:
Before we pray through the things weighing on our hearts, let's journal and pray through God's agenda first — declaring that we want His will to be done in us and through us more than anything else. We want His will in every relationship and every area of our lives. When we trade our will for God's will, we are stepping into true surrender.

3. "GIVE US THIS DAY OUR DAILY BREAD." (Matthew 6:11)

When Jesus taught us what to pray each day, His first request from God the Father was for daily bread. The Greek word for "daily," *epiousion* (ἐπιούσιον), can be best understood as referring to the present of today, here and now, as well as the days to come.

NOTE FROM JOEL

The image of bread in Scripture was developed even further by Jesus as He instituted Communion, (Luke 22:14-20) which reminds us of the Passover in the Old Testament. (Exodus 12:1-28) When we observe Communion today and break the bread, we are reminded of the body of Jesus — the One who sustains us, who redeemed us through the breaking of His own body.

As we read through the Bible, we can be on the lookout for other examples of images or ideas in the Old Testament that were shadows of something to come in the New Testament. The sacrificial system of an unblemished lamb, for instance, finds its fulfillment in Jesus, the Lamb of God, who is without sin yet took on the sin of humanity on the cross.

We see a variety of forms of bread in the Bible. In the Old Testament, it came as a loaf (Leviticus 2:4) and as manna from heaven. (Deuteronomy 8:3) Bread was a daily provision from God. (Exodus 16:4) But most importantly, in the New Testament, Jesus called Himself the Bread of Life. (John 6:35) And one day, God promises we will receive bread at the heavenly banquet. (Luke 22:16; Isaiah 25:6)

So the mention of bread in the Lord's Prayer is not just intended for us to pray in hopeful anticipation for the future (the heavenly banquet) but also to pray as we are sustained by God's perfect provision in the present (manna).

It can feel exhausting to rely on God's provision when it's just not coming yet ... when we've asked for a solution to our problems and our pain but we haven't seen the manna we want. But if God's provision isn't as we expected, then we must trust there's something God knows that we don't know. Even when what we see in front of us feels confusing. Even when what we see in front of us isn't at all what we thought it would look like. Even when we don't agree that this is good. We can trust Him.

PRAY:
Use the space below to journal and pray through things you need, and even just desire, from God. And then trust Him for those answers in His perfect timing. Remember, friend, Jesus is the Bread of Life. He is the most miraculous provision and the One already given to us today.

4. "AND FORGIVE US OUR DEBTS, AS WE ALSO HAVE FORGIVEN OUR DEBTORS." (Matthew 6:12)

For someone living during the time of Jesus, hearing the word "debt" would have stirred up many emotions. In those days, the weight of power within the government caused the overwhelming majority of people to be borrowers, not lenders. They knew what it was like to be under the burdensome weight of unpayable debt. What joy, what peace, what freedom, to know that Jesus had come to pay all their spiritual debt!

Even as Christians today, when we are reminded that we have been cleared of the debt of our sin because of the blood of Jesus Christ, it should cause us to jump for joy! And it should cause us to desire freedom and forgiveness for others too.

... Yes, even that person. You know, the one who used to be one of our closest friends, but now we feel an awkward distance. Or the one who spoke those cruel words that sometimes still replay in our heads at night. Or that family member we have a strained relationship with. However the word "forgiveness" makes you feel in light of hard relationships you may be facing, we understand. And so does Jesus.

Forgiving doesn't mean the wrong done is no longer wrong. Forgiving doesn't always mean everything is forgotten, like nothing ever happened. And you don't have to conquer the whole forgiveness journey today with that person. But today is a great opportunity to simply sit with the Lord and consider what forgiveness could look like. In this relationship. In your own heart. What would it look like to cooperate with the forgiveness Jesus has given to you and extend it to another person?

PRAY:
Use the space below to thank God for the free gift of His forgiveness. As you consider anything you yourself need to confess and ask God to forgive, also ask God: *Who is someone I need to forgive?* Invite His help as you begin that process today.

5. "AND LEAD US NOT INTO TEMPTATION, BUT DELIVER US FROM EVIL." (Matthew 6:13)

Temptation is a part of our human experience. Even Jesus was tempted. But before Jesus died, He promised the Holy Spirit would come to help us stand firm against the lure of sin. (John 14:25-27) So today, when we put our faith in Jesus, we are given the Holy Spirit to help us fight against our sin nature, the snares of the world and the designs of Satan.

Galatians 5:19-24 shows us that in our flesh, we would choose a life focused on ourselves: *"Now the works of the flesh are evident: sexual immorality, impurity, sensuality, idolatry, sorcery, enmity, strife, jealousy, fits of anger, rivalries, dissensions, divisions, envy, drunkenness, orgies, and things like these. I warn you, as I warned you before, that those who do such things will not inherit the kingdom of God. But the fruit of the Spirit is love, joy, peace, patience, kindness, goodness, faithfulness, gentleness, self-control; against such things there is no law. And those who belong to Christ Jesus have crucified the flesh with its passions and desires."*

Thanks to Jesus, we don't have to live as slaves to our sin.

PRAY
To close out the Lord's Prayer, pray from the place of victory we have as believers, and take your stand against the enemy. Spiritual warfare can seem like a complex or intimidating topic — but it doesn't have to paralyze our prayers. God hears us when we simply ask for His protection against temptation and the schemes of the evil one. We can trust Him to handle everything this means.

NOTES

NOTES

NOTES

NOTES

ENDNOTES

WHAT IS PRAYER?

[1] Montgomery, James. "Prayer is the soul's sincere desire," hymn, 1818.

[2] Hardin, Leslie T. "Prayer." *The Lexham Bible Dictionary*, Lexham Press, 2016.

[3] Okholm, Dennis L. "Prayer." *Evangelical Dictionary of Biblical Theology,* Baker Reference Library. Baker Book House, 1996, p. 622.

[4] Elwell, Walter A. and Barry J. Beitzel. "Prayer." *Baker Encyclopedia of the Bible,* Baker Book House, 1988, p. 1745.

[5] Kapic, Kelly M. and Wesley Vander Lugt. *Pocket Dictionary of the Reformed Tradition,* The IVP Pocket Reference Series. IVP Academic, 2013, p. 88.

[6] Hatchett, Randy. "Prayer." *Holman Illustrated Bible Dictionary*, Holman Bible Publishers, 2003, p. 1320.

HOW TO BUILD A HABIT OF PRAYER

[1] Graham, B. *Hope for the Troubled Heart.* Bantam Books, 1993, p. 146.

FUN FACTS ABOUT THE PSALMS

[1] STEP stands for "Scripture Tools for Every Person" and is designed to give users across the world, particularly those in disadvantaged countries, free access to trustworthy Bible expertise. Created by Bible scholars at Tyndale House (Cambridge, UK), it is curated by a nondenominational body of scholars and other volunteers who are passionate about sharing accurate information on the Bible.

WEEK ONE

DAY 1

[1] Allen P. Ross, *The Bible Knowledge Commentary: An Exposition of the Scriptures,* 1985, 1, p. 895.

DAY 2

[1] "Q. If the Milky Way was the size of a coffee cup, how big would the rest of the universe be?" National Aeronautics and Space Administration, edited by Nancy Bray, August 3, 2017, https://www.nasa.gov/centers/kennedy/about/information/science_faq.html.

[2] Kidner, Derek. P*salms 1–72: An Introduction and Commentary,* InterVarsity Press, Downers Grove, IL, 1973.

DAY 3

[1] Muddamalle, Joel. Excerpted from forthcoming book with W Publishing (HarperCollins Christian Publishing), releasing spring 2024.

DAY 4

[1] Kidner, Derek. *Psalms 73–150: An Introduction and Commentary*, InterVarsity Press, Downers Grove, IL, 1975.

[2] Guthrie, Donald. *Hebrews: An Introduction and Commentary,* InterVarsity Press, Downers Grove, IL, 1983.

WEEK TWO

DAY 6

[1] Hamilton Jr., James M. *Psalms Volume I: 1-72 Evangelical Biblical Theology Commentary,* edited by T. Desmond Alexander, Thomas R. Schreiner, and Andreas J. Köstenberger, 2021.

DAY 8

[1] Kidner, Derek. Qtd. in "Psalm 38." *The Enduring Word Bible Commentary by David Guzik*, 2020, https://enduringword.com/bible-commentary/psalm-38/.

WEEK THREE

DAY 13

[1] Baumol, Avi (2009). "Psalm 100: Mizmor l'Todah". *The Poetry of Prayer: Tehillim in Tefillah*. Gefen Publishing House Ltd.

[2] Allen P. Ross, *The Bible Knowledge Commentary: Old Testament*. Colorado Springs: David C Cook, 1985, p. 865.

DAY 14
[1] Allen P. Ross, *The Bible Knowledge Commentary: Old Testament.* Colorado Springs: David C Cook, 1985, p. 871.

DAY 15
[1] Allen P. Ross, *The Bible Knowledge Commentary: Old Testament.* Colorado Springs: David C Cook, 1985, p. 891.

WEEK FOUR

DAY 16
[1] Boga, Matt. "L(amen)ting with Hope." The Gospel Coalition, May 15, 2020. https://www.thegospelcoalition.org/article/lamenting-with-hope/

DAY 17
[1] Brooks, Page and D. A. Neal. "Theodicy." *The Lexham Bible Dictionary*, Bellingham, WA, Lexham Press, 2016.

[2] Horne, Thomas Hartwell. Cited in "Psalm 10 – From Times Of Trouble To Calm Confidence." *The Enduring Word Bible Commentary by David Guzik,* 2020. https://enduringword.com/bible-commentary/psalm-10/

DAY 18
[1] Piper, John. "Death Rehearsal," excerpted from "I Have Kept the Faith," desiringGod, December 28, 1980. https://www.desiringgod.org/articles/death-rehearsal

[2] Guzik, David. "Psalm 90 – The Prayer Of Moses In The Wilderness." *The Enduring Word Bible Commentary by David Guzik,* 2020. https://enduringword.com/bible-commentary/psalm-90/

DAY 19
[1] Walter A. Elwell and Barry J. Beitzel, "Music and Musical Instruments," *Baker Encyclopedia of the Bible,* Grand Rapids, MI, Baker Book House, 1988. p. 1506.

[2] Ramsey, K.J. "Scripture and Neuroscience Agree: It Helps to Lament in Community." *Christianity Today,* November 15, 2019. https://www.christianitytoday.com/ct/2019/november-web-only/neuroscience-and-scripture-agree-it-helps-to-lament-in-comm.html

WEEKEND REFLECTION
[1] Nicoll, William R. "Commentary on Psalms 22." *The Expositor's Bible Commentary.* https://www.studylight.org/commentaries/eng/teb/psalms-22.html.

WEEK FIVE

DAY 21
[1] Spurgeon, Charles. Cited in "Psalm 37 – Wisdom Over Worry." *The Enduring Word Bible Commentary by David Guzik,* 2020. https://enduringword.com/bible-commentary/psalm-37/

DAY 22
[1] Boice, James Cameron. Cited in "Psalm 17 – Wisdom Over Worry." *The Enduring Word Bible Commentary by David Guzik,* 2020. https://enduringword.com/bible-commentary/psalm-17/

DAY 23
[1] Spurgeon, Charles. Cited in "Psalm 143 – Hope for the Persecuted Soul." The Enduring Word Bible Commentary by David Guzik, 2020. https://enduringword.com/bible-commentary/psalm-143/

WEEK SIX

JESUS CHRIST: THE GREAT INTERCESSOR
[1] Spurgeon, Charles. "Intercessory Prayer." *Metropolitan Tabernacle Pulpit Volume 7,* August 11, 1861. https://www.spurgeon.org/resource-library/sermons/intercessory-prayer-2/#flipbook/

[2] Spurgeon, Charles. "Intercessory Prayer." *Metropolitan Tabernacle Pulpit Volume 7,* August 11, 1861. https://www.spurgeon.org/resource-library/sermons/intercessory-prayer-2/#flipbook/

DAY 27
[1] Henry, Matthew. "Complete Commentary on Psalms 60:10." *Henry's Complete Commentary on the Whole Bible,* 1706, https://www.studylight.org/commentaries/mhm/psalms-60.html

DAY 28
[1] Kidner, Derek. Cited in "Psalm 20 – The Lord Saves His Anointed." *The Enduring Word Bible Commentary by David Guzik,* 2020. https://enduringword.com/bible-commentary/psalm-20/

[2]"עֹנִי" *Brown-Driver-Briggs Hebrew and English Lexicon,* Unabridged. Electronic Database, Biblesoft, Inc., 2006. https://biblehub.com/hebrew/6030.htm

DAY 29

[1] Spurgeon, Charles. "A Sacred Solo." *Spurgeon's Sermons Volume 24: 1878*, https://ccel.org/ccel/ spurgeon/sermons24/sermons24.

about
PROVERBS 31
MINISTRIES

She is clothed with strength and dignity;
she can laugh at the days to come.

PROVERBS 31:25

Proverbs 31 Ministries is a nondenominational, nonprofit Christian ministry that seeks to lead women into a personal relationship with Christ. With Proverbs 31:10-31 as a guide, Proverbs 31 Ministries reaches women in the middle of their busy days through free devotions, podcast episodes, speaking events, conferences, resources, Online Bible Studies and training in the call to write, speak and lead others.

We are real women offering real-life solutions to those striving to maintain life's balance, in spite of today's hectic pace and cultural pull away from godly principles.

Wherever a woman may be on her spiritual journey, Proverbs 31 Ministries exists to be a trusted friend who understands the challenges she faces and walks by her side, encouraging her as she walks toward the heart of God.

Visit us online today at proverbs31.org!

PROVERBS 31
ministries

YOUR NEXT STUDY IS ALMOST HERE!

JOIN US FOR ...

Right Where You're Supposed To Be:

A STUDY OF THE BOOK OF ESTHER

AVAILABLE SEPTEMBER 2023
AT P31BOOKSTORE.COM